Smart CHOICE

Smart learning—your way, every day.

STUDENT BOOK

2

KEN WILSON

OXFORD
UNIVERSITY PRESS

OXFORD
UNIVERSITY PRESS

Great Clarendon Street, Oxford, OX2 6DP, United Kingdom

Oxford University Press is a department of the University of Oxford. It furthers the University's objective of excellence in research, scholarship, and education by publishing worldwide. Oxford is a registered trade mark of Oxford University Press in the UK and in certain other countries

First published in 2020
2024
10

ISBN: 978 0 19 406114 8 Student Book with Online Practice Pack
ISBN: 978 0 19 406115 5 Student Book Component
ISBN: 978 0 19 406108 7 Student Online Practice

Printed in Great Britain by Bell and Bain Ltd, Glasgow

This book is printed on paper from certified and well-managed sources

ACKNOWLEDGEMENTS

Front cover photograph: (selfie/FatCamera), (Asian Woman/ jhorrocks)

Illustrations by: 5W Infographics pp.81, 85, 97; Dani Germenia/Beehive Illustration p.13; Infomen/Début Art pp.9, 49; Eda Kaban/Shannon Associated pp.21, 89, 92, 101, 104; Greg Paprocki p.13; Geo Parkin/António Adrião Artist Representative pp.4, 32, 36, 46, 56, 66, 76, 95, 107; Gavin Reece/New Division pp.7, 10, 33, 70; Joseph Taylor/Mendola Art pp.2, 30, 47; Laszlo Veres/Beehive Illustration p.44; Terry Wong p.39.

The Publishers would like to thank the following for their kind permission to reproduce photographs and other copyright material: 123rf: pp.16 (6/germanskydiver), 19 (snowboarding/Dmytro Vietrov), 33 (grapes/nikkiphoto), (mistletoe/Oleksandr Rybitskyi), 36 (salad/yelenayemchuk), 41 (yawning/anetlanda), 68 (Lady Gaga headshot/yelo34); Alamy: pp.8 (zip line/Yadid Levy), (tarzan swing/Stefano Paterna), 15 (Millie Bobby Brown/UPI), 16 (2/Lilyana Vynogradova), (5/David Crane), (7/Andi Duff), 19 (whitewater rafting/Michele Oenbrink), (cave diving/cbpix), 20 (El Capitan/Polly Thomas), 24 (8/Steve Bloom Images), 27 (B/John Warburton-Lee Photography), (C/Jon Arnold Images Ltd), 28 (electric bus/travellinglight), (bicycle lane/Natallia Khlapushyna), 35 (carnival/Pulsar Imagens), (birthday celebration/Tony Tallec), 39 (ping pong/GoGo Images Corporation), 41 (headache/DCPhoto), 43 (woman/Fancy), 53 (Connie/Eugenio Marongiu), 55 (woman/AY Media AS), 60 (damaged car/moodboard), 61 (music performer/dpa picture alliance), 64 (3/Michael Dwyer), (4/MBI), (5/Aleksei Gorodenkov), 67 (making models/TongRo Images), (grandmother/Jon Arnold Images Ltd), 74 (polluted beach/Jack Sullivan), (clean beach/Nigel Cattlin), 75 (train/maximimages.com), 79 (audio producer/Paul Vasarhelyi), 87 (students/Vadym Drobot), (row of restuarants/Chris Hellier), 88 (dragon boat race/CHINA Landmarks and People by Vision), (close up of dragon boat/Imaginechina Limited), (contestants rowing/Jayne Russell), 90 (Chatuchak weekend market/Ivan Nesterov), 99 (students/Vadym Drobot), (row of restuarants/Chris Hellier), 100 (dragon boat race/CHINA Landmarks and People by Vision), (close up of dragon boat/Imaginechina Limited), (contestants rowing/Jayne Russell), 102 (Chatuchak weekend market/Ivan Nesterov), 108 (woman on laptop/DCPhoto), (college student/Aflo Co., Ltd.), 113 (man/Stefan Dahl Langstrup); Getty: pp.6 (male tourist/Westend61), 7 (art class/sanjeri), (Chinese class/RedChopsticks), (acting class/CasarsaGuru), 15 (people watching movie/John Eder), 16 (4/simonkr), 20 (Alex Honnold portrait/Jay L. Clendenin), 23 (female hiker/Michael DeYoung), 29 (Wellington/José Fuste Raga), (Cairo/Leonid Andronov), 33 (lucky bags/RUNSTUDIO), 50 (1/Michael Heim/EyeEm), (2/Mikolette), (3/Mango Productions), (4/antikainen), (5/kali9), 59 (women canoeing/Yuji Ozeki), (woman jetskiing/YanLev), 61 (crowd/Steve Russell), (car collision/Yellow Dog Productions/The Image Bank), 64 (2/Hill Street Studios), (6/fstop.123), 67 (collecting stamps/Silent Resilience Photography), (climbing trees/Cyndi Monaghan), 73 (woman radio interview/Nicola Katie), 75 (car/Andy Lyons), 79 (space engineer/Hero Images), 80 (building library/Stephen Buwert), 91 (Danielle/John Lund/Marc Romanelli/Blend Images/Corbis), (Yukiko/Tetra Images), (Antonio/Jack Hollingsworth/Photodisc), 94 (eco house in Honduras/JOSE CABEZAS/Stringer), (eco house in Yelwa/AFP/Stringer), 103 (Danielle/John Lund/Marc Romanelli/Blend Images/Corbis), (Yukiko/Tetra Images), (Antonio/Jack Hollingsworth/Photodisc), 106 (eco house in Honduras/JOSE CABEZAS/Stringer), (eco house in Yelwa/AFP/Stringer), 109 (Denver/Darryl Brooks/EyeEm), 110 (family party/Thomas Barwick), 111 (woman/Pattanasit Sangsuk/EyeEm); Newcom: p.93 (Venus and Serena Williams/Robert Deutsch/ZUMA Press)

Oxford University Press: pp.16 (3/Shutterstock/Mirelle), 24 (2/Shutterstock), (4/Shutterstock/jakobradlgruber), (6/Shutterstock; e2dan), 28 (windfarm/Shutterstock/ssuaphotos), 43 (flowers/Shutterstock), 75 (plane/Dejan Milinkovic), 80 (shark/Shutterstock; frantisekhojdysz), 91 (Andrea/Stockbyte), 103 (Andrea/Stockbyte); Shutterstock: pp.4 (tent/Alexlukin), 10 (film reel/Steve Collender), 12 (festival/Andriy Solovyov), 14 (stunt performer/JanBeZiemi), 16 (climbing gear/swinner), (1/Melinda Nagy), (8/Vasily Smirnov), 20 (Alex Honnold climbing/J Chin/National Geographic/Kobal), 24 (pyramids/WitR), (1/AerialVision_it), (3/Sadik Yalcin), (5/aimpol buranet), (7/Yusnizam Yusof), (9/Harvepino), (10/Maksimilian), 27 (A/Szakharov), 30 (balloons/Andrey Armyagov), 34 (lanterns/Sakdawut Tangtongsap), (kites/Komar), (painted elephant/Thavorn Rueang), 35 (winter walking/Alexander Rochau), 39 (meditation/wavebreakmedia), (t'ai chi/Nadya Lukic), 40 (depressed teen/fizkes), 44 (hat/Lifestyle Travel Photo), 50 (magnifying glass/Room's Studio), 54 (person being interviewed/Dean Drobot), 55 (man/Andresr), 56 (colorful band aids/Anton Starikov), 59 (man waterskiing/leedsn), 61 (pickpocket/mrkornflakes), 63 (panda mascot/kipgodi), 64 (stage mask/Viorel Sima), (1/Just2shutter), 68 (Lady Gaga with cup and suacer/Beretta/Sims/Karius), 70 (drinks bottles/New Africa), 74 (bird/Amit Shankar Pal), 75 (bicycle/Pixel-Shot), 76 (lifebuoy/Photology1971), 79 (fashion designer/wavebreakmedia), 80 (tortoise/9MOT), 83 (couple cycling/Odua Images), 86 (beach volleyball/lazyllama), 87 (baseball/mTaira), 90 (Kel K bazaar/Alex Azabache), 91 (Hans/baranq), (Isabel/Nicotombo), (Adam/aremafoto), (Bruce/Eugene F), 98 (woman bungee jumping/Pumpchn), 99 (baseball/mTaira), 102 (Kel K bazaar/Alex Azabache), 103 (Hans/baranq), (Isabel/Nicotombo), (Adam/aremafoto), (Bruce/Eugene F), 105 (John Cho/Helga Esteb), 109 (hispanic man/AJR_photo), (asian man/Mina Tkla), 111 (Chinatown/f11photo), (fortune cookie/Mark Carrel), 112 (fire engine/IGOR GALLO KALASSA); Third Party: p.48 (Retuna shopping mall/Lina Östling/Retuna), (customers at Retuna/Lina Östling/Retuna).

New for

Smart CHOICE

Smart learning—your way, every day.

Welcome to *Smart Choice* Fourth Edition. Here's how you can get more involved in your *Smart Choice* lessons:

PRESS PLAY

Watch and learn with **conversation videos** that bring everyday English into each unit.

Feel confident in your learning and explore topics and ideas from around the world with **documentary videos.**

Download all videos from *Smart Choice* at **smartchoice4e.oxfordonlinepractice.com** for access in class, at home, and on the move. Get started with the access code in the front of your book.

GET SPEAKING

OVER TO YOU ACTIVITIES

Have fun learning with new **Over to You** activities! Use the support on the Conversation and Speaking pages to create your own dialogues in English.

SPEAKING AND SMART TALK

Speaking and **Smart Talk** pages in each unit let you practice what you learn with quizzes, games, and real-life situations.

BONUS UNITS

Practice your speaking skills with activities after each video in the **Bonus Units**.

3 OVER TO YOU Find out about a green project in your town or city. Share the information with the class.

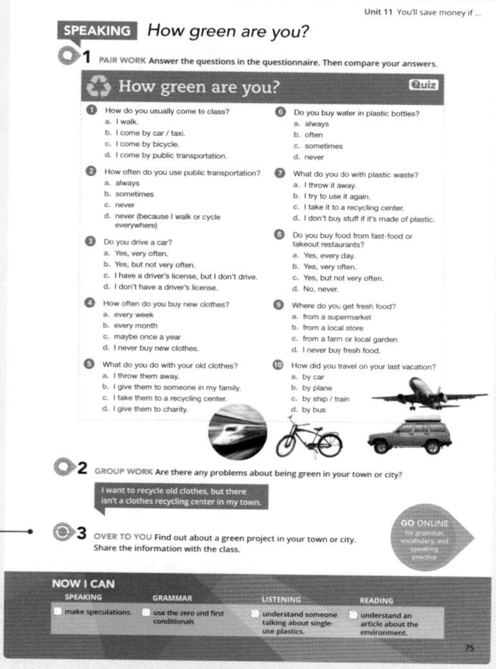

Unit 11 You'll save money if ...

SPEAKING *How green are you?*

1 PAIR WORK Answer the questions in the questionnaire. Then compare your answers.

How green are you? Quiz

1. How do you usually come to class?
   a. I walk.
   b. I come by car / taxi.
   c. I come by bicycle.
   d. I come by public transportation.
2. How often do you use public transportation?
   a. always
   b. sometimes
   c. never
   d. never (because I walk or cycle everywhere)
3. Do you drive a car?
   a. Yes, very often.
   b. Yes, but not very often.
   c. I have a driver's license, but I don't drive.
   d. I don't have a driver's license.
4. How often do you buy new clothes?
   a. every week
   b. every month
   c. maybe once a year
   d. I never buy new clothes.
5. What do you do with your old clothes?
   a. I throw them away.
   b. I give them to someone in my family.
   c. I take them to a recycling center.
   d. I give them to charity.
6. Do you buy water in plastic bottles?
   a. always
   b. often
   c. sometimes
   d. never
7. What do you do with plastic waste?
   a. I throw it away.
   b. I try to use it again.
   c. I take it to a recycling center.
   d. I don't buy stuff if it's made of plastic.
8. Do you buy food from fast-food or takeout restaurants?
   a. Yes, every day.
   b. Yes, very often.
   c. Yes, but not very often.
   d. No, never.
9. Where do you get fresh food?
   a. from a supermarket
   b. from a local store
   c. from a farm or local garden
   d. I never buy fresh food.
10. How did you travel on your last vacation?
    a. by car
    b. by plane
    c. by ship / train
    d. by bus

2 GROUP WORK Are there any problems about being green in your town or city?

I want to recycle old clothes, but there isn't a clothes recycling center in my town.

3 OVER TO YOU Find out about a green project in your town or city. Share the information with the class.

GO ONLINE for grammar, vocabulary, and speaking practice

NOW I CAN

SPEAKING	GRAMMAR	LISTENING	READING
make speculations.	use the zero and first conditionals	understand someone talking about single-use plastics.	understand an article about the environment.

75

SCOPE AND SEQUENCE

UNIT	VOCABULARY	CONVERSATION	LANGUAGE PRACTICE AND PRONUNCIATION
Useful classroom language PAGES 2–3	Key phrases for classroom interaction and learning		
01 How was your vacation? PAGES 4–9 	**Vacation activities**	▶ Where did you stay? **Over to you:** Ask your partner about his / her vacation.	**Grammar:** Agreeing with *so* and *neither*; disagreeing **Pronunciation:** Word stress
02 I think it's boring! PAGES 10–15 	**Movies and music**	▶ I'm not really interested. **Over to you:** Make plans related to movies and music.	**Grammar:** Adjectives ending in *-ing* and *-ed* **Pronunciation:** Final *-ed* sounds
03 Do it before you're 30! PAGES 16–21 	**Extreme sports and activities**	▶ I've never done anything! **Over to you:** Ask your partner about his / her personal experiences.	**Grammar:** The present perfect **Pronunciation:** Linked sounds
BONUS Units 1–3 PAGES 22–23	▶ How to make money and travel full-time Talk about countries to visit and activities to do there.		
04 The best place in the world! PAGES 24–29 	**Natural features**	▶ Have you been there? **Over to you:** Talk about where you want to go and why.	**Grammar:** Superlative adjectives **Pronunciation:** Reduction of *t*
05 Where's the party? PAGES 30–35 	**Special events**	▶ I'm going to a wedding! **Over to you:** Talk about plans for a celebration.	**Grammar:** Adverbial clauses: *before*, *after*, and *when* **Pronunciation:** Intonation of adverbial clauses
06 You should try it! PAGES 36–41 	**Healthy and unhealthy activities**	▶ I have to study! **Over to you:** Refuse an invitation with a reason.	**Grammar:** *should* and *have to* **Pronunciation:** Reduction of *have to* and *has to*
BONUS Units 4–6 PAGES 42–43	▶ A Cocos Malay wedding Talk about wedding experiences and customs.		

LISTENING	READING & WRITING	SPEAKING	NOW I CAN
Talking about vacation classes	**Reading:** Zip-lining in Costa Rica **Writing:** An email about vacation preferences (p. 108)	*What did you do on vacation?* **Smart Talk:** *How are you different?* (pp. 84, 96)	• Describe a vacation • Agree and disagree with others • Understand activities and plans • Understand an article about an unusual vacation
Interviewing people who work in movies and music	**Reading:** Action men (and women) **Writing:** A blog post about movies (p. 108)	*You and the movies* **Smart Talk:** *What's interesting and what's boring?* (pp. 85, 97)	• Understand and give opinions • Use *-ing* and *-ed* adjectives • Understand interviews about making movies and music • Understand an article about stunt performers
Talking about personal experiences for a job application	**Reading:** Have you ever seen anything like this?: Alex Honnold **Writing:** An email about your country (p. 109)	*Find someone who has ...* **Smart Talk:** *Have you ever ... ?* (pp. 86, 98)	• Talk about personal experiences • Use the present perfect • Understand conversations about personal experiences • Understand an article about free climbing
People taking part in a quiz	**Reading:** Where are the greenest places on earth? **Writing:** An email about your city (p. 109)	*Geography quiz!* **Smart Talk:** *The superlative quiz* (pp. 87, 99)	• Describe places • Use superlative adjectives • Understand a geography game show • Understand an article about green places
New Year's traditions	**Reading:** Festival time in Asia **Writing:** A description of a party (p. 110)	*My favorite months* **Smart Talk:** *Dragon boats* (pp. 88, 100)	• Descirbe special cultural events • Use clauses with *before*, *after*, and *when* • Understand different New Year's traditions • Understand an article about Asian festivals
Advice for people who want to change their lifestyles	**Reading:** Do you have low self-esteem? **Writing:** An email about a class (p. 110)	*Living a healthy lifestyle* **Smart Talk:** *Help! Is this true?* (pp. 89, 101)	• Make suggestions and talk about obligations • Use *should* and *have to* • Understand people giving advice • Understand an article about self-esteem

SCOPE AND SEQUENCE

UNIT	VOCABULARY	CONVERSATION	LANGUAGE PRACTICE AND PRONUNCIATION
07 There are too many stores! PAGES 44–49 	**Things to buy**	It was too expensive. **Over to you:** Ask about a recent shopping trip.	**Grammar:** *too / not enough*; *too many / too much* **Pronunciation:** Word stress in complaints
08 Wanted: People who can sing PAGES 50–55 	**Describing personality**	I'm trying to find a job. **Over to you:** Talk about applying for a vacation job.	**Grammar:** Defining relative clauses **Pronunciation:** Word stress and content words
09 What were you doing? PAGES 56–61 	**Accidents and injuries**	What happened to you? **Over to you:** Talk about an accident or injury you had.	**Grammar:** The past continuous **Pronunciation:** Linked sounds with /y/
BONUS Units 7–9 PAGES 62–63	Sophie's costume Talk about dressing up for a charity event		
10 I used to sing. PAGES 64–69 	**School activities and clubs**	You're really good! **Over to you:** Talk about what you used to do when you were younger.	**Grammar:** *used to* **Pronunciation:** Linking and vowel reduction in *used to*
11 You'll save money if … PAGES 70–75 	**Recycling**	Things might get better! **Over to you:** Order something from your partner.	**Grammar:** Zero and first conditionals **Pronunciation:** Word stress in conditional sentences
12 You could be a lifeguard. PAGES 76–81 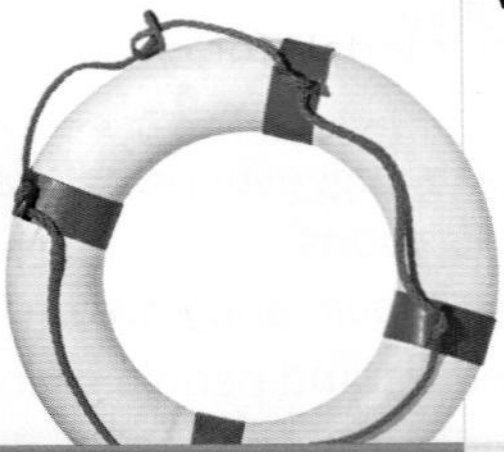	**Vacation jobs**	You must be worried. **Over to you:** Talk about applying for a job.	**Grammar:** Modals for possibility, speculation, and deduction **Pronunciation:** Reduction of *must be*, *can't be*, and *might be*
BONUS Units 10–12 PAGES 82–83	A biofuelled trip Talk about being green on vacation		

LISTENING	READING & WRITING	SPEAKING	NOW I CAN
People talk about shopping habits	**Reading:** A different kind of shopping mall **Writing:** A blog about your favorite place to shop (p. 111)	*A shopping game* **Smart Talk:** *Shopper's paradise?* (pp. 90, 102)	• Make complaints and discuss shopping • Use *too, enough, many, much* • Understand conversations about shopping habits • Understand an article about an unusual mall
Phone conversation about house-sitting	**Reading:** How to impress an interviewer **Writing:** An email about you and your preferences (p. 111)	*The most important thing to me* **Smart Talk:** *Making connections* (pp. 91, 103)	• Describe my preferences • Use relative clauses for description • Understand voicemail messages about house-sitting • Understand an article about interview tips
People describe an accident	**Reading:** Six-year-old boy drives mom's car to school! **Writing:** A paragraph about something that happened to you (p. 112)	*Have you ever ...?* **Smart Talk:** *What happened?* (pp. 92, 104)	• Narrate past events • Use the past continuous • Understand descriptions of accidents • Understand an article about a dramatic event
People talk about their family history	**Reading:** Ten things you didn't know about Lady Gaga **Writing:** Comments on a website about past habits (p. 112)	*Find someone who used to ...* **Smart Talk:** *Before they were famous* (pp. 93, 105)	• Talk about past habits • Use *used to* • Understand family histories • Understand a short biography about a famous person
Radio interview about single-use plastics	**Reading:** And now the good news! **Writing:** An email about a local environmental problem (p. 113)	*How green are you?* **Smart Talk:** *Making houses from plastic bottles* (pp. 94, 106)	• Make speculations • Use the zero conditional, first conditional, and *if* clauses with *may* or *might*. • Understand someone talking about single-use plastics • Understand an article about the environment
Talking about study and career plans	**Reading:** A volunteer vacation **Writing:** An email about living in your country (p. 113)	*What next?* **Smart Talk:** *What are your plans?* (pp. 95, 107)	• Talk about future plans • Use modals for possibility, speculation and deduction • Listen to people talking about careers and studying abroad • Understand a text about volunteering on vacation

Useful classroom language

VOCABULARY

1 **Listen and repeat.**

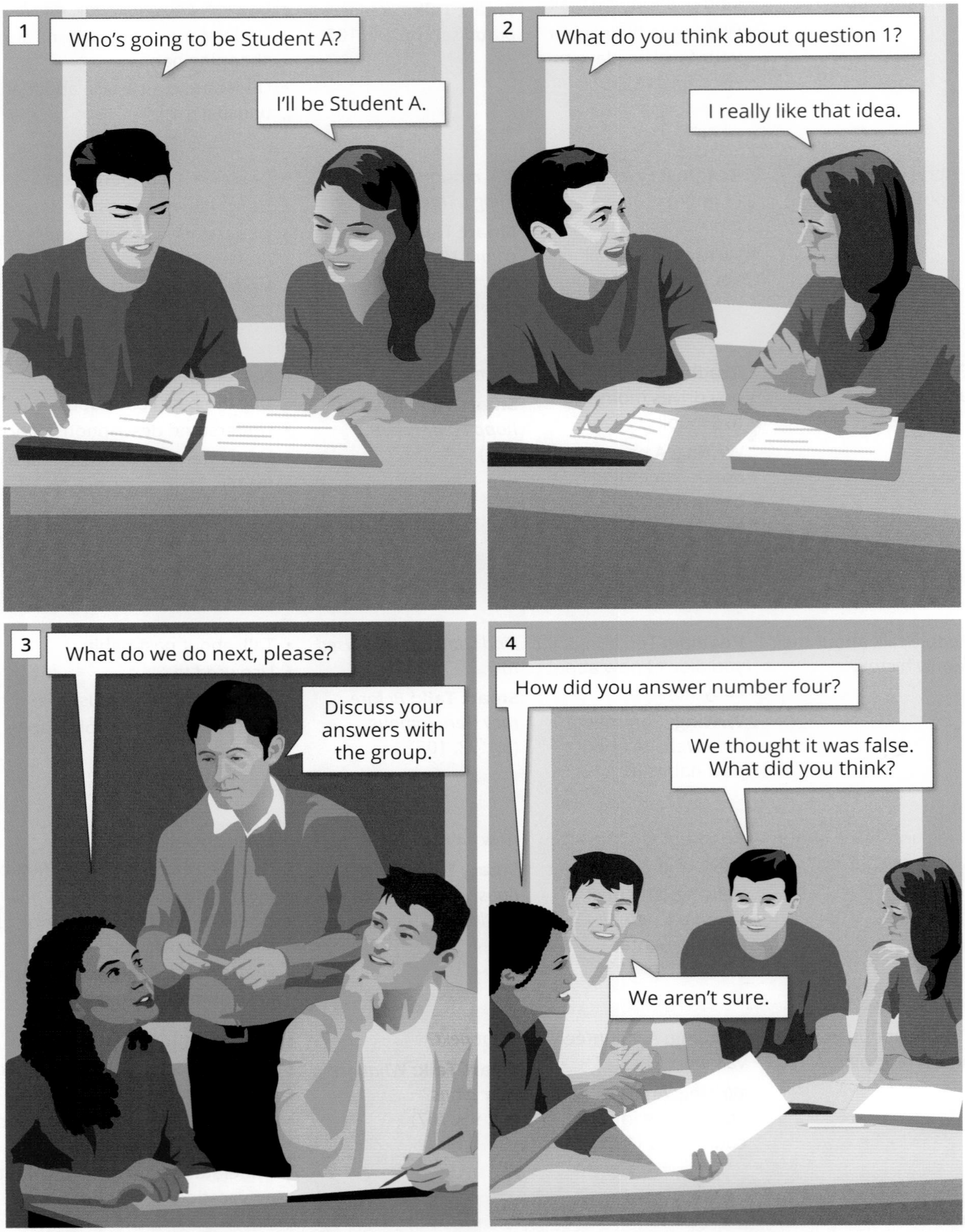

CONVERSATION

1 **Complete the conversations with the phrases in the box. Then watch and check your answers.**

Can I ask you something?	Do you want to speak for the group?
What does "popular" mean?	How did you answer the first one?
Did you do your homework?	Can you explain it again, please?

1. A Can I ask you something?
   B Sure.
   A I don't understand this one.
   ____

2. A ____________________
   B For number 1, I wrote "not enough."
   A Really? I wrote "too much"!

3. A ____________________
   B No, but Maria took some notes.
   A OK, I'll ask her.

4. A ____________________
   B Yes, but I didn't do question 5.
   ____
   A It means a lot of people like it.
   B Thanks!

2 PAIR WORK **Practice the conversations with a partner.**

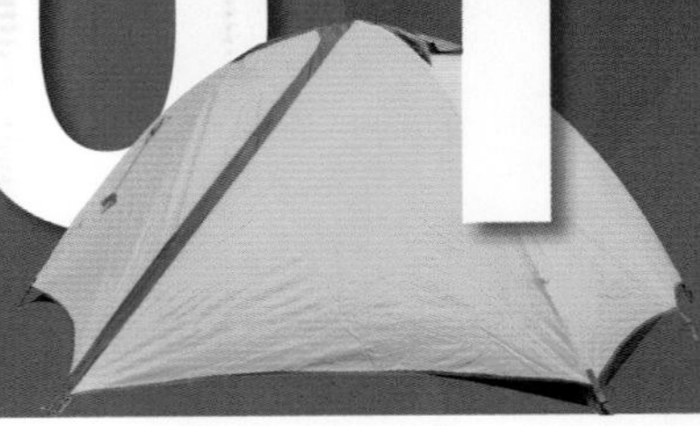

01 How was your vacation?

SPEAKING
Vacations
GRAMMAR
Agreeing / Disagreeing
LISTENING
Activities and plans
READING
Unusual vacation article

WARMUP
What was your favorite vacation?

VOCABULARY

1 Look at the pictures. What are the activities? Write the correct letter. Then listen and check your answers.

a. rock climbing	d. camping	g. whitewater rafting
b. hiking	e. surfing	h. visiting museums
c. sightseeing	f. kayaking	i. scuba diving

2 **PAIR WORK** Which activities above did you do in the past? Which activities do you want to do? Tell your partner.

I went kayaking last year.

Really? How was it?

It was great! I want to go surfing.

Me, too!

VOCABULARY TIP

Make flashcards to learn new words.

surfing

standing on board in the water

CONVERSATION

1 Complete the conversation. Then watch and check your answers. Practice the conversation with a partner.

a. kayaking b. by a river c. campground d. studied

Adam	Hi, Maria! How was your summer vacation?
Maria	It was OK. I **1** ______ most of the time.
Adam	So did I. I didn't have money for a real vacation.
Maria	Neither did I. But I spent one weekend **2** ______ .
Adam	Really? So did I. Where did you stay?
Maria	I was at a **3** ______ called "The Falls."
Adam	No way! So was I!
Maria	Really? That's strange—I didn't see you. What did you do there?
Adam	I went **4** ______ .
Maria	Hey! So did I! I loved it.
Adam	Really? I didn't. It was hard work!
Maria	Oh, that's a pity.

2 PAIR WORK Practice the conversation again. Use the ideas below. Add your own ideas.

1	2	3	4
worked	in a forest	hostel	hiking
stayed home	at the beach	beach resort	whitewater rafting
______	______	______	______

3 OVER TO YOU Work in pairs. Make a video of your conversation. Ask your partner about his / her vacation.

Student A	Ask Student B about his / her vacation. Compare it with your vacation.
Student B	Answer Student A's questions. Talk about your vacation.

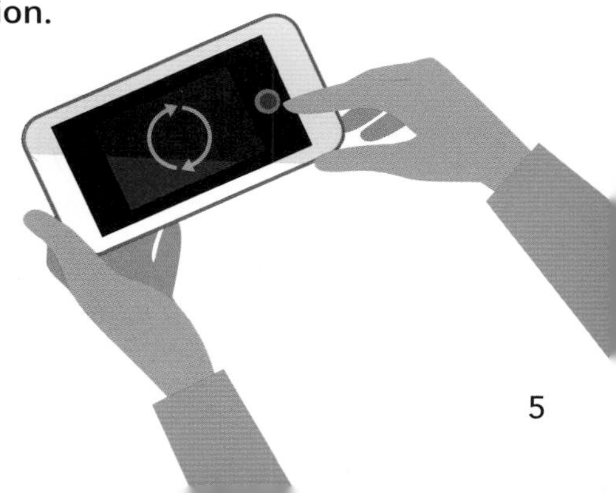

LANGUAGE PRACTICE

Agreeing and disagreeing

Grammar Reference page 114

	Agree	Disagree
I**'m** going on vacation.	**So am** I.	Really? I**'m not**.
I **was** at the beach.	**So was** I.	Oh, I **wasn't**.
I **like** hiking.	**So do** I.	Really? I **don't**.
I **stayed** at a nice hotel.	**So did** I.	I **didn't**.
I**'m not** going on vacation.	**Neither am** I.	Really? I **am**.
I **don't** want to go camping.	**Neither do** I.	Well, I **do**.
I **can't** take a vacation this year.	**Neither can** I.	Oh, I **can**.

1 **Match the statements and responses.**

1. I didn't take a vacation this year. _e_
2. I want to visit Europe next year. ____
3. He doesn't want to go scuba diving. ____
4. I'm planning to go sightseeing. ____
5. I can't go on the trip. ____
6. We went kayaking. ____

a. Neither can I.
b. So did we!
c. Really? I'm not.
d. Oh, I do.
e. Neither did I.
f. So do I.

2 **Complete the conversations. Agree or disagree.**

1. A I want to travel to different countries.
   B ______________________ . It's the best thing to do.
2. A I'm not going to the beach this year.
   B ______________________ . I'm going to the mountains.
3. A I want to visit the Grand Canyon one day.
   B ________________ ? ________________ . I like visiting cities.
4. A I don't like doing sports on vacation.
   B ________________ ? ________________ . It's boring sitting around doing nothing.

3 PAIR WORK **Respond to the statements in activity 2 with information about you.**

I want to travel to different countries.

Really? I don't. I want to spend my vacations here.

PRONUNCIATION *Word stress*

1 **Listen. Notice the stress on subject words when agreeing or disagreeing.**

1. I was at the beach yesterday. So was I!
2. I like swimming. Really? I don't.
3. Jo can't play the guitar. Well, Rob can.
4. I don't have a car. Neither do I.

2 **Listen again and repeat. Be sure to stress the subject words correctly.**

LISTENING

1 **BEFORE YOU LISTEN** **Look at the photos. Do you take evening or vacation classes? Do you think the classes in the photos are interesting?**

art class

Chinese class

acting class

2 **Listen to two students talking about their vacation. Write *T* (Tim) and / or *J* (Jane) next to the places they visited and the subjects they mention.**

1. Italy ____
2. San Francisco ____
3. acting ____
4. art ____
5. grandparents ____
6. languages ____
7. Italian ____
8. Portuguese ____
9. Chinese ____

3 **Listen again. Answer the questions.**

1. What does Jane want to study this semester? ______________________
2. Where do Tim's grandparents live? ______________________
3. What did he also do when he visited them? ______________________
4. What did he do at the end of his classes? ______________________
5. What did Tim and Jane finally agree about the vacation? ______________________

4 **LISTENING PLUS** **Listen to a conversation between Tim, Jane, and Lisa. Choose (✓) *True* or *False*.**

	True	False
1. Lisa recognized Tim when she saw him.	☐	☐
2. Tim and Lisa were in the same class last semester.	☐	☐
3. Lisa and Jane met in Europe this summer.	☐	☐
4. Lisa's grandparents live in Italy.	☐	☐
5. Lisa saw Tim in San Francisco.	☐	☐

SMART TALK ***How are you different?*** **Student A:** Turn to page 84.
Student B: Turn to page 96.

READING

1 BEFORE YOU READ **Look at the photos. What are the people doing?**

The Monteverde Extremo zip line

ZIP-LINING IN COSTA RICA

If you're looking for an adventure vacation, this is it! In Costa Rica, there are zip lines over the rainforests. A zip line is a **cable**. Costa Rica has the longest zip line in Latin America, the Monteverde Extremo, which is 1,590 meters long. Parts of it are more than 400 meters above the ground, and there are 14 **platforms**. You stand on the platform, attach yourself to the cable, and fly down the zip line over the trees! There is also a Tarzan **swing**. You can hold onto a rope and swing over a **valley**. It looks really dangerous. I can't imagine doing something like this. I'm not very **athletic**.

My friend Amy called me about three months ago. "Do you have any vacation plans this year?" she asked.

"No, I don't," I replied.

"OK, neither do I. But I have an idea."

I love Amy, but she's a problem. When she discovers something new, she wants to do it. And she wants me to do it with her. This year, she discovered zip-lining.

"I think we should go to Costa Rica," she said.

"I'm afraid of **heights**," I said.

"So am I," said Amy.

"I want to go to the beach on vacation and do nothing," I said.

"No, you don't," she said.

Now here we are in Costa Rica. Today we rode on the Monteverde Extremo and the Tarzan swing. They were really **frightening**, but a great thing to do! I recommend them to everyone.

The Tarzan swing

2 **Read the article. Answer the questions.**

1. When did the writer get a call from Amy?
2. Was he enthusiastic about Amy's idea?
3. What was his alternative suggestion?
4. Describe the Monteverde Extremo.
5. In the end, how did he feel about the experience?

3 GROUP WORK **Discuss the questions with your group.**

1. Is there anything like this experience in your country?
2. Do you want to do something like this?

I think it's a great idea.

So do I. I'd like to do it.

WRITING Turn to page 108.

SPEAKING *What did you do on vacation?*

1 PAIR WORK Follow the instructions to play the board game.

- Write numbers 1 to 9 on pieces of paper and put them in a bag or box.
- Take a number and ask your partner about the activity on the board.
- Respond to your partner's answer, agreeing or disagreeing, and ask for more information.
- Take turns asking questions. Make notes of your partner's information.

Did you study on your vacation?

No, I didn't.

Neither did I. So, what did you do?

I went to the beach.

2 GROUP WORK Join another pair. Tell the group about your partner's vacation. Ask for more information about the other students' vacations.

Rita went to Rio last summer. She went sightseeing.

Rita, did you go to Copacabana Beach?

3 OVER TO YOU Find an unusual and interesting activity to do on vacation. Share the information with the class.

GO ONLINE for grammar, vocabulary, and speaking practice

NOW I CAN

SPEAKING	GRAMMAR	LISTENING	READING
☐ describe a vacation.	☐ agree and disagree with others.	☐ understand activities and plans.	☐ understand an article about an unusual vacation.

02 I think it's boring!

SPEAKING
Giving opinions
GRAMMAR
-ing / *-ed* adjectives
LISTENING
Making movies and music
READING
Stunt performers article

WARMUP
What movie do you want to see?

VOCABULARY

1 Look at the pictures. What are the movie styles? Write the correct letter. Then listen and check your answers.

a. action movie
b. animation
c. romantic comedy
d. martial arts movie
e. horror movie
f. science fiction movie
g. Bollywood movie
h. musical
i. documentary

2 **PAIR WORK** What kinds of movies do you like? Ask your partner.

A Do you like action movies?
B Yes, I do.
A So do I!

B Do you like horror movies?
A No, I don't.
B Neither do I.

CONVERSATION

1 **Complete the conversation. Then watch and check your answers. Practice the conversation with a partner.**

a. a horror movie **b.** rock music **c.** frightening **d.** college

Ricardo	Hey, Amy. Where are you?
Amy	I'm at the **1** __________. Do you want to come and see a movie?
Ricardo	It depends. What is it?
Amy	It's **2** __________.
Ricardo	Oh, come on! You know I don't like them. They're so **3** __________.
Amy	No, you'll like this one. It's funny.
Ricardo	I'm not really interested in movies.
Amy	I know that! You prefer listening to boring **4** __________.
Ricardo	I don't think it's boring.
Amy	Well, I do. So, do you want to come and see this movie with me?
Ricardo	Well, maybe next time.

2 PAIR WORK **Practice the conversation again. Use the ideas below. Add your own ideas.**

1	2	3	4
movie theater	an action movie	violent	soul music
library	a romantic comedy	boring	rap
________	________	________	________

3 OVER TO YOU **Work in pairs. Make a video of your conversation. Make plans related to movies or music.**

Student A	Invite Student B to a movie. Agree with Student B where to go.
Student B	When you can't agree, make another suggestion.

CONVERSATION TIP

BEING POLITE

When you can't agree, try to make other suggestions.

Do you want to come?

Well, maybe next time.

LANGUAGE PRACTICE

Adjectives ending in *-ing* and *-ed* Grammar Reference page 115

I think horror movies are **frightening**.
They're **frightening** movies.

I'm **frightened by** horror movies.

I think action movies are **interesting**.
They're **interesting** movies.

I'm **interested in** action movies.

Do you like classical music?
Yes, it's very **relaxing**.
I'm **relaxed** when I listen to it.

Do you like watching movies in movie theaters?
No. I think other people are **annoying**.
No. I'm **annoyed by** other people.

1 Complete the sentences with a pair of words.

amazed—amazing	excited—exciting
bored—boring	disappointed—disappointing

1. Her new track is _amazing_ ! I'm _amazed_ by her voice! How does she make that sound?
2. I'm ___________ about this weekend. Going to a concert is really ___________ !
3. That's ___________ ! I'm really ___________ the concert is sold out.
4. This music is so ___________ ! I always get ___________ when I listen to jazz.

2 Complete the adjectives in the questions.

1. Do you think classical music is relax______ ?
2. Are you tir______ today?
3. What's an interest______ TV show to watch?
4. Are you interest______ in science fiction?
5. What do you think is an amaz______ movie?

3 PAIR WORK Ask and answer the questions in activity 2.

Do you think classical music is relaxing?

No. I'm more relaxed when I listen to rock music.

PRONUNCIATION *Final -ed sounds*

1 Listen. Notice how the final *-ed* sounds like /d/, /t/, or /ɪd/. What sound does each word end with? Choose the correct sound.

1. bored /d/ /t/ /ɪd/
2. relaxed /d/ /t/ /ɪd/
3. interested /d/ /t/ /ɪd/
4. frightened /d/ /t/ /ɪd/
5. excited /d/ /t/ /ɪd/

2 Listen again and repeat. Be sure to say the final *-ed* sound correctly.

LISTENING

1 **BEFORE YOU LISTEN Look at the pictures. What are the people in red doing? Label each picture with an activity from the box.**

play in a band	direct a movie	record a song	act in a movie

A. ______ B. ______ C. ______ D. ______

2 **Listen to four interviews. Number the pictures above.**

3 **Listen again. Choose the correct ending to the sentences.**

1. Sandra is going to ____ .
   a. act in a horror movie **b.** direct a horror movie
2. She's planning to do it ____ .
   a. at a beach house **b.** in a movie studio
3. Alison is going to ____ .
   a. direct the movie with Sandra **b.** appear in the movie
4. She plays the part of ____ .
   a. a police officer **b.** the monster's victim
5. Andy can play ____ .
   a. piano and guitar **b.** guitar and violin
6. He wants to ____ .
   a. start his own band **b.** tour with a famous band
7. Briana and Enrique ____ .
   a. write songs together **b.** sing songs together
8. Next week, they're going to record their songs ____ .
   a. on a computer **b.** in a studio

4 **LISTENING PLUS Listen to more interviews with the people in activities 2 and 3. Answer the questions.**

1. What problem did Sandra have when they made the movie? ______
2. How did the actors feel about the movie? ______
3. Why was Andy disappointed? ______
4. What was the problem in the studio for Briana and Enrique? ______
5. Which of the five people want to try the activity again? ______

SMART TALK ***What's interesting and what's boring?*** **Student A:** Turn to page 85. **Student B:** Turn to page 97.

READING

1 **BEFORE YOU READ** **What do you know about stunt performers in action movies?**

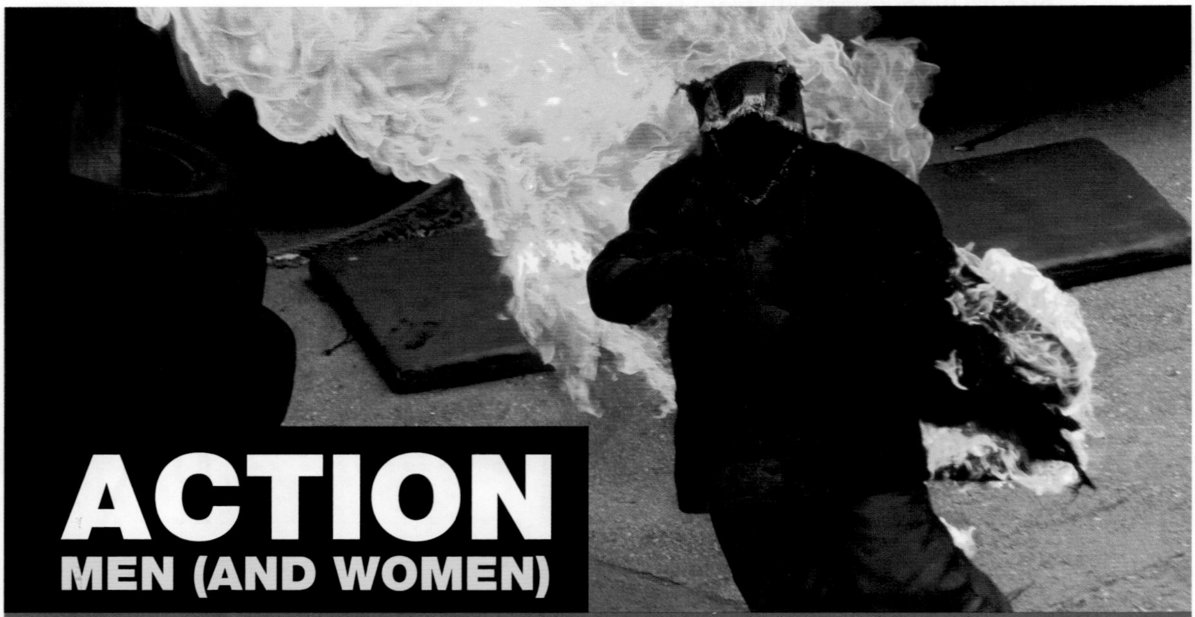

ACTION
MEN (AND WOMEN)

Sharon Starr is a stunt performer. She works on US TV cop shows. One day, she wants to work in Hollywood movies.

How did you start working as a stunt performer?
About ten years ago, I was working as an **extra** on a TV show, and I met two stuntmen. There was a fire in a house, and one of them ran out with his clothes on fire. I was really **impressed**!

I found out about a school for stunt performers, and I did a course there. I got my first stunt job three months after I finished the course, on a **comedy show**!

Things are different now, and as well as men, there are a lot of women stunt performers.

Is it dangerous?
Stunt organizers are very good, and the planning is amazing. But the performers have to **concentrate**. If the planning is good, it isn't dangerous. But if you don't concentrate, it can be very dangerous.

Is the money good?
Every job is different. Stunt performers in Hollywood **blockbusters** can make a lot of money. A guy jumped off the CN Tower in Toronto and got $150,000. The jump took ten seconds—that's $15,000 per second for the job! But, of course, if you're hurt, you can't work or make any money.

Did you have any serious accidents?
I broke my arm once. It was only my second job, and I jumped through a window. It wasn't a real glass window, so it didn't hurt. Unfortunately, my shoulder hit the window frame and I fell 30 meters to the ground. I was really angry at myself for making a mistake.

2 **Read the text and answer the *yes/no* questions. Give more information.**

1. Does Sharon only want to work on TV?
2. Did Sharon get her first stunt job on a TV cop show?
3. Is stunt work always dangerous?
4. Do all stunt performers make a lot of money?
5. Did Sharon break her arm because of the glass?

3 **PAIR WORK** **Think of three good things and three bad things about a stunt performer's job. Talk to your partner. Are your lists similar?**

WRITING Turn to page 108.

SPEAKING *You and the movies*

1 PAIR WORK Why do you go and see a new movie? Choose (✓) one or more of the reasons. Then discuss your reasons with your partner.

☐ the poster ☐ the reviews ☐ the trailer ☐ your friends' opinions

2 Complete the survey with information about you.

MOVIE SURVEY

1 How often do you watch a movie?
a. every week
b. never
c. once a month
d. other ______________________

2 Where do you prefer to watch movies?
a. in a movie theater
b. on television
c. on your computer
d. on your tablet/phone

3 In a movie theater, do you …
a. watch the credits at the end of the movie?
b. always eat and drink the same things?
c. get annoyed by other people (e.g., looking at their phones)?

4 Which movies do you prefer to watch? Why?
a. local movies
b. movies in another language
c. movies in English
d. other ______________________

5 Who are your favorite actors? Why?
Male: ______________________
Female: ______________________

6 What's your favorite movie? Why?
____

3 GROUP WORK Compare your answers. Who is similar to you?

How often do you watch a movie?

I usually watch one every week. What about you?

I never watch movies!

4 OVER TO YOU Find three reviews of one of your favorite movies. Describe them to the class. Which do you agree with?

GO ONLINE for grammar, vocabulary, and speaking practice

NOW I CAN

SPEAKING	GRAMMAR	LISTENING	READING
☐ understand and give opinions.	☐ use *-ing* and *-ed* adjectives.	☐ understand interviews about making movies and music.	☐ understand an article about stunt performers.

03 Do it before you're 30!

SPEAKING
Personal experiences
GRAMMAR
Present perfect
LISTENING
Applying for a job
READING
Free climbing article

WARMUP
Do you like extreme sports?

VOCABULARY

1 Look at the photos. What are the extreme sports and activities? Write the correct letter. Then listen and check your answers.

a. bungee jumping	**d.** parasailing	**g.** BASE jumping
b. driving a race car	**e.** BMX bike racing	**h.** skydiving
c. ice climbing	**f.** wingsuit flying	

1 *a*

2 ___

3 ___

4 ___

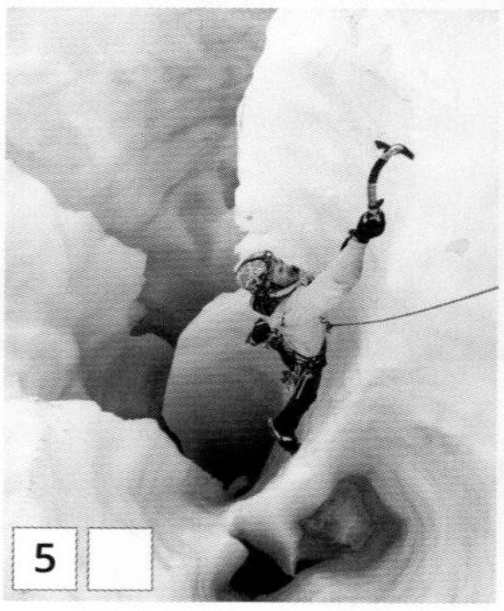
5 ___

6 ___

7 ___

8 ___

2 PAIR WORK Which things in the pictures do you want to try? Compare your answers.

Do you want to try ice climbing?

Yes, I do. Do you want to try wingsuit flying?

No, I don't.

Why not?

It's frightening.

VOCABULARY TIP

Make word associations to learn new words.

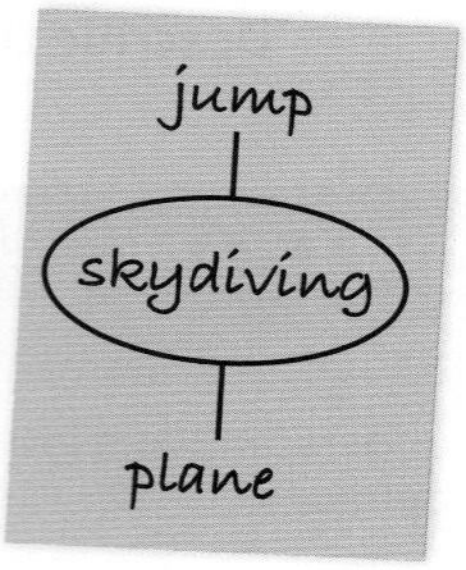

CONVERSATION

1 **Complete the conversation. Then watch and check your answers. Practice the conversation with a partner.**

a. washed the dishes b. a BMX bike c. a race car d. skydiving

Maria	Have you read this article, "Things to Do before You're 30"?
Amy	No, I haven't. What's it about?
Maria	It's a list of things to try. For example, have you ever ridden **1** ________ ?
Amy	No, I haven't.
Maria	Neither have I. The next question is: have you ever driven **2** ________ ?
Amy	No, I haven't.
Maria	OK. Question three: have you ever been **3** ________ ?
Amy	No, I haven't. I've never done anything!
Maria	That's not true! You've done a lot of things. They're just not on this list.
Amy	By the way, have you ever **4** ________ ?
Maria	No, I haven't.
Amy	Do you want to start now? I'm really busy.

2 PAIR WORK **Practice the conversation again. Use the ideas below. Add your own ideas.**

1	2	3	4
a motorcycle	a sports car	BASE jumping	cleaned the windows
a horse	an electric car	hang-gliding	done the laundry
________	________	________	________

3 OVER TO YOU **Work in pairs. Make a video of your conversation. Ask your partner about his / her personal experiences.**

Student A	Ask Student B about an experience.
Student B	Answer Student A and compare your experiences.

LANGUAGE PRACTICE

The present perfect

Grammar Reference page 116

Have you ever **ridden** a motorcycle?
Yes, I **have**. I rode one yesterday.
No, I **haven't**. But **I've ridden** a bicycle.

Has she ever **driven** a sports car?
Yes, she **has**. She drove one on vacation.
No, she**'s** never **driven** a car.

Have you ever **been*** skydiving?
Yes, I **have**. I went last summer.
No, I **haven't**. But I've **been** parasailing.

* *been* is another past participle form of *go*

1 PAIR WORK Complete the conversations. Then practice them with a partner.

1. A Have you ever *eaten* Moroccan food? (eat)
   B Yes, I ________ . I ________ it in France. (try)
2. A Have you ever ________ windsurfing? (go)
   B Yes, I ________ . I ________ last year. (go)
3. A Have you ever ________ a movie star? (meet)
   B No, I ________ . But my sister ________ Emma Stone once. (see)
4. A Have you ever ________ a marathon? (run)
   B No, but I ________ to catch a bus this morning! (run)

REGULAR VERBS
jump → jumped
play → played
visit → visited
try → tried
IRREGULAR VERBS
be → been
buy → bought
do → done
drive → driven
eat → eaten
fly → flown
go → gone / been
meet → met
ride → ridden
run → run
see → seen

2 PAIR WORK Write sentences about you. Then compare them with a partner.

1. (ride a horse) *I've never ridden a horse. / I rode a horse last summer.*
2. (go to Europe) ________
3. (see an elephant) ________
4. (fly in an airplane) ________

3 PAIR WORK Answer the questions in activity 1 with information about you.

Have you ever eaten Moroccan food?

No, I haven't. Is it good?

PRONUNCIATION *Linked sounds*

1 Listen. Notice how consonant sounds link to words that begin with vowel sounds.

1. Have you ever ridden a horse?
2. Have you ever bought a car?
3. Have you ever run a marathon?
4. Have you ever seen an elephant?

2 Listen again and repeat. Be sure to link the words.

LISTENING

1 BEFORE YOU LISTEN **Look at the photos. Have you ever tried the activities? Can you do them in your area?**

snowboarding

whitewater rafting

cave diving

2 **Listen to a phone conversation between two friends. Choose the best summary.**

a. Marco doesn't know how to answer a question on an application.

b. Marco has done some extreme sports.

c. Marco can't remember what activities he has done.

3 **Listen again. Choose (✓) *True* or *False*.**

	True	False
1. Marco has never traveled outside the US.	☐	☐
2. He once went skydiving in Colorado.	☐	☐
3. Anya wants to try cave diving.	☐	☐
4. Marco's parents have never been to Florida.	☐	☐
5. Marco went cave diving when he was ten.	☐	☐

4 LISTENING PLUS **Listen to a second conversation between Marco and Anya. Answer the questions.**

1. What news does Marco have about the job? ____________________

2. What is the first thing he's worried about? ____________________

3. What does Anya tell him to do? ____________________

4. What is the second thing Marco is worried about? ____________________

5. What does he like about Anya? ____________________

SMART TALK ***Have you ever ... ?***
Student A: Turn to page 86.
Student B: Turn to page 98.

READING

1 **BEFORE YOU READ** **What do you think El Capitan is? And what do you think Alex Honnold does?**

Have you ever seen anything like this?

1. Free solo climbing

Q: What is free solo climbing?

Free solo climbing is a form of rock climbing. The climber climbs alone, without ropes or other equipment. It is very dangerous. Only 1% of climbers try it.

Q: Who is Alex Honnold?

He's one of the best free solo climbers in the world. On June 3, 2017, he did a free solo climb of El Capitan.

Q: What is El Capitan?

It's a **vertical rock formation** in Yosemite National Park, California. It's about 3,200 feet high (more than 900 meters). Someone once said, "Climbing El Capitan is like climbing glass."

Q: How many times has Alex Honnold climbed El Capitan?

He climbed El Capitan more than 40 times with ropes and a partner before he tried it free solo.

2. Filming the climb

Free Solo is the film of Alex Honnold's climb of El Capitan. It won the Oscar for best documentary in 2019. A climber named Jimmy Chin and his wife Elizabeth Chai Vasarhelyi directed it.

There were a lot of challenges making the film. First of all, people can't use **drones** in Yosemite. So the directors needed **camera operators** with experience in both filming and climbing. The crew filmed Honnold on El Capitan for two years before the climb, when he was practicing with ropes. The camera operators often had to climb quickly ahead of Honnold and be careful not to get in each other's **shots**.

Sound was a problem, too. They wanted to hear Honnold **breathing**, as well as the sounds of his hands and feet on the cliff, but he didn't want to wear a **microphone** on his back. They put it in his **bag of chalk** instead.

Free Solo is one of the most exciting documentaries about climbing. Go and see it!

2 **Read the article. Correct the information in the statements.**

1. About half of climbers try free solo climbing.
2. Honnold practiced for two weeks before doing the free solo climb of El Capitan.
3. *Free Solo* won the Oscar for best movie in 2019.
4. The camera operators used drones for the filming.
5. Honnold didn't want to wear a microphone on his ankle.

3 **GROUP WORK** **Discuss the questions.**

1. Which words do you think describe free solo climbers and what they do? Why?

a. brave **b.** crazy **c.** dangerous **d.** exciting **e.** other: ___________

2. Do you want to try something like this? Why or why not?

I think these people are crazy!

So do I. I don't want to try something like that.

WRITING Turn to page 109.

SPEAKING *Find someone who has …*

1 Look at the questions in the survey. Add two more activities to the list.

Have you ever …	Name	Extra information
1 run a marathon?		
2 tried bungee jumping?		
3 taken dance lessons?		
4 flown in a helicopter?		
5 won an award?		
6 sung in public?		
7 visited another country?		
8 written a poem?		
(your choice) ________________ ?		
(your choice) ________________ ?		

2 CLASS ACTIVITY Ask classmates the survey questions. Write the names of students who say "yes." Try to get extra information!

Have you ever run a marathon?

Yes, I have. I ran a marathon last year.

Where did you do it?

In New York City.

3 GROUP WORK Choose the best story from your group. Share the story with the class.

Eric ran a marathon in New York City last year. It was really exciting …

4 OVER TO YOU Find out about an extreme sport that you find interesting. Share the information with the class.

GO ONLINE for grammar, vocabulary, and speaking practice

NOW I CAN

SPEAKING	GRAMMAR	LISTENING	READING
☐ talk about personal experiences.	☐ use the present perfect.	☐ understand conversations about personal experiences.	☐ understand an article about free climbing.

VIDEO

How to make money and travel full-time

1 PAIR WORK Look at the pictures. How are the people traveling? Why do you think they travel full-time? Discuss your answers with your partner.

2 Watch the video. Check (✓) the activities you see.

- ☐ cooking
- ☐ driving
- ☐ eating
- ☐ hiking
- ☐ ice climbing
- ☐ riding a bike
- ☐ rowing
- ☐ scuba diving
- ☐ skydiving
- ☐ whitewater rafting

CULTURE TIP

People usually give boats a name. Many boat owners believe that you should never change a boat's name, because it will bring bad luck.

3 Watch the video again. Complete the sentences with one word from the video.

1. Bee and Theo started traveling in ____________ .
2. They travel around in their narrowboat and ____________ .
3. Theo thinks it's important to work from where you are ____________ .
4. Bee and Theo make money from ____________ , filmmaking, and social media.
5. Theo says it's important to create a nice-looking ____________ .
6. They have an online ____________ , so they can sell prints of Theo's photos.
7. For their podcasts, they ____________ people who have different lifestyles.

4 PAIR WORK Write two countries you'd like to visit and an activity you'd like to do there. Discuss your answers with a partner.

Country	Activity
1.	
2.	

I'm really interested in going to China.

So am I. What would you like to do there?

I want to go sightseeing and see the Great Wall.

So do I. That would be amazing.

READING

1 PAIR WORK Look at the photo. What kind of vacation do you think the woman likes?

STUDENTS ON THE GO

This week's "Student on the Go" is 20-year-old Lauren Walker from Dublin in Ireland. We interviewed Lauren about her plans for the summer.

Where are you spending your summer vacation this year?
I'm going to Cape Cod, in the US, for three months. I've never been to the States before, so I'm really excited about it. I've seen a couple of travel documentaries about Cape Cod, and it looks amazing.

What are you going to do over there?
I've got work at a campground. I've always loved camping and being outdoors. I enjoy meeting new people, too, so I think it'll be a really interesting job.

What are you going to do when you aren't working?
I want to spend time kayaking and sailing. I love being on the water; it's so relaxing. I also want to go sightseeing, of course! I'm really interested in history and art, and I've heard there are lots of good museums and galleries to visit.

Have you ever had a working vacation before?
Yes, I have. Last year, I spent July and August working in Queenstown, in New Zealand. It was my summer vacation, but of course, it was winter there! I had a great time. I went snowboarding during the day and then worked as a server in a restaurant in the evenings. I also tried bungee jumping for the first time. It was quite frightening, but very exciting!

Do you usually travel by yourself?
Yes, I do. A lot of people think it's boring to travel alone, but I don't. I actually prefer it. I've been on vacation a few times with friends, but I sometimes get annoyed traveling with a group. It's difficult to choose things to do that everyone likes and keep everyone happy. When I travel by myself, I can do what I want, when I want!

2 Read the article. Answer the questions.

1. How long is Lauren going to spend in the US?
2. Which sports does Lauren mention?
3. Why does Lauren want to visit museums and galleries?
4. What was Lauren's job last summer?
5. Does Lauren prefer traveling alone or with friends? Why?

3 GROUP WORK Discuss the questions.

1. How do students in your country usually spend their summer vacation?
2. Would you like to have a working vacation? Why / Why not?
3. Do you prefer traveling alone, with friends, or with family? Why?

04 The best place in the world!

SPEAKING
Describing places
GRAMMAR
Superlative adjectives
LISTENING
Geography game show
READING
Green places article

WARMUP
What is the most beautiful place in your country?

VOCABULARY

1 Look at the photos. Match them with the words in the box. Write the correct letter. Then listen and check your answers.

a. island	c. continent	e. lake	g. rainforest	i. desert
b. ocean	d. mountain range	f. river	h. waterfall	j. volcano

1 *e*

2 ___

3 ___

4 ___

5 ___

6 ___

7 ___

8 ___

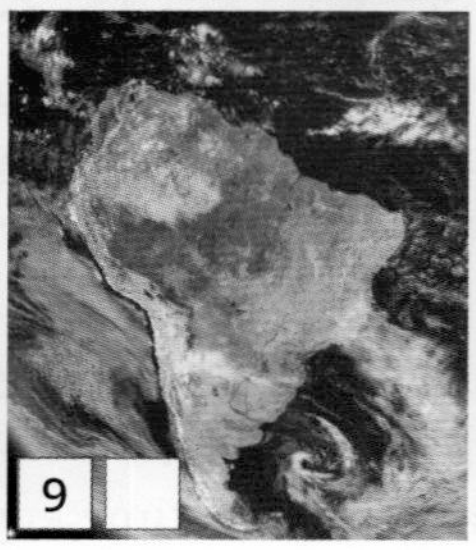
9 ___

10 ___

2 **PAIR WORK** Complete the chart with places you know. Then compare your chart with a partner.

Oceans	Rainforests	Waterfalls	Islands
Lakes	**Mountain ranges**	**Deserts**	**Rivers**

What did you write for "Oceans"?

I wrote *Pacific*.

Do you know anything about the Pacific Ocean?

CONVERSATION

1 **Complete the conversation. Then watch and check your answers. Practice the conversation with a partner.**

a. island **b.** Chile **c.** Easter Island

Scott	So, where are you from, Rosa?
Rosa	I'm from **1** ______ .
Scott	Really? I've always wanted to go there.
Rosa	That's nice to hear. Any reason?
Scott	I really want to visit **2** ______ . Have you been there?
Rosa	Of course! It's one of the most popular places in my country.
Scott	What's it like?
Rosa	It's amazing! I think it's the most beautiful **3** ______ in the world!
Scott	Well, I want to go there someday.
Rosa	I hope you get the chance.
Scott	Me, too!

2 **PAIR WORK** **Practice the conversation again. Use the ideas below. Add your own ideas.**

1	2	3
Peru	the Andes	mountain range
Thailand	Bangkok	city
______	______	______

3 **OVER TO YOU** **Work in pairs. Make a video of your conversation. Talk about where you want to go and why.**

Student A Say a place you want to go and why.
Student B Ask follow-up questions. Then say a place you want to go and why.

CONVERSATION TIP

ASKING QUESTIONS
Ask follow-up questions to extend the conversation.

It's very popular.

Why do people like it?

LANGUAGE PRACTICE

Superlative adjectives	Grammar Reference page 117
Which ocean is larger, the Atlantic or the Pacific?	The Pacific is larger than the Atlantic. The Pacific is **the largest** ocean in the world.
What is **the biggest** desert in the world?	The Sahara is **the biggest** desert in the world.
Which city is **the most beautiful**: Venice, Florence, or Rome?	I think Venice is **the most beautiful** city!
NOTE: good → better → **the best** bad → worse → **the worst**	

1 Complete the sentences with superlative adjectives. Use the words in the box.

cold deep dry large

1. Lake Baikal is the deepest lake in Russia.
2. Is Australia ________________ island in the world, or is it a continent?
3. Is the Arctic ________________ place on Earth?
4. I think the Atacama Desert is ________________ place on the planet.

2 Complete the conversations. Use the adjectives in parentheses.

1. **A** What's ________________ city in China? (big)
   B I think it's Chongqing, isn't it?
2. **A** Is the Grand Prismatic ________________ spring in Yellowstone? (hot)
   B I really don't know, but it's certainly ________________. (colorful)
3. **A** Is the Andes ________________ mountain range in the world? (long)
   B I think so, but ________________ mountains are in the Himalayas. (tall)
4. **A** What are ________________ forests on the planet? (important)
   B The rainforests, right?
5. **A** Is Lake Titicaca ________________ lake in the world? (clear)
   B I don't think so. But it's definitely ________________. (high)

PRONUNCIATION *Reduction of* t

1 Listen. Notice how the final *t* can be reduced when words ending in *st* are followed by a consonant sound.

Unreduced		Reduced and linked	
the largest city	/ðə lɑrdʒɪst 'sɪti/	the larges(t) city	/ðə lɑrdʒɪs 'sɪti/
the driest place	/ðə draɪɪst 'pleɪs/	the dries(t) place	/ðə draɪɪs 'pleɪs/
the best way	/ðə best 'weɪ/	the bes(t) way	/ðə bes 'weɪ/
the most beautiful	/ðə moʊst 'byutɪfl/	the mos(t) beautiful	/ðə moʊs 'byutɪfl/

2 Listen again and repeat. Try to say the reduced sounds and link the adjectives and nouns.

LISTENING

1 BEFORE YOU LISTEN **Look at the photos. Which continents are these places on? Label the photos with *Africa*, *Antarctica*, or *North America*.**

A. ____________

B. ____________

C. ____________

2 **Listen to the college quiz show. As you listen, choose the answer you think is correct.**

1. **a.** Africa **b.** Asia **c.** North America
2. **a.** Africa **b.** Asia **c.** North America
3. **a.** Europe **b.** Antarctica **c.** Australia
4. **a.** Africa **b.** Antarctica **c.** Australia
5. **a.** New York City **b.** Los Angeles **c.** Mexico City

3 **Listen again. Answer the questions.**

1. How many people live in Asia? ____________________
2. How many countries are there in Africa? ____________________
3. Where is the largest subtropical desert in the world? ____________________
4. How many people live in North America's largest city? ____________________

4 LISTENING PLUS **Listen to more of the quiz. Choose the correct answer.**

1. In the second round, the teams ____ .
   a. must answer six questions
   b. choose a number to get a question
2. The first question is about the world's longest river, and ____ .
   a. both teams give the right answer
   b. both teams give the wrong answer
3. The second question is about ____ .
   a. the highest mountains in the Himalayas
   b. the location of the Himalayas
4. The San Francisco team wins because ____ .
   a. they know where Aconcagua is
   b. they know that Argentina is in South America

SMART TALK ***The superlative quiz*** **Student A:** Turn to page 87.
Student B: Turn to page 99.

READING

1 **BEFORE YOU READ** Look at the photos. Where are the greenest places in your country?

WHERE ARE THE GREENEST PLACES ON THE PLANET?

All over the world, there are problems with climate change and air pollution, but there is also lots of GOOD NEWS.

- **Vancouver, Canada**, is the greenest city in North America. Almost all of the city's electricity is from **renewable sources**, including **hydroelectric dams** and wind power. They also encourage local food production, so less food comes from other parts of the world by plane or ship.
- **Curitiba, Brazil**, is possibly the greenest city in South America. There are more than 400 square kilometers of **green space**. There is also a very good transportation system, and most people travel by bus.
- **China** produces more wind power than any other country. The largest **onshore wind farm** in the world is in Gansu Province in northwest China. China also has more **electric buses** than any other country, and the city of **Shenzhen** has the most of any city—more than 16,000.
- The largest numbers of people using public transportation are, of course, in the world's biggest cities. Eight million passengers a day take the subway in **Seoul**. Even more people use the **Tokyo urban rail system**—8.66 million!
- **Copenhagen, Denmark** is the most bike-friendly city in the world. Nearly half of the city's workers bike to work. There are nearly 400 kilometers of **bike lanes**, including a 20-kilometer Cycle Super Highway.

electric bus

onshore wind farm

bike lane

2 Read the article. Match the places with the green ideas.

1. Seoul / Tokyo
2. Shenzhen
3. Copenhagen
4. Vancouver

a. more electric buses than any other city
b. a special highway for bikers
c. more local food production
d. most people using public transportation

3 **PAIR WORK** Which of the ideas in the reading text are a good idea for your city / town? Discuss with your partner.

I think bike lanes are a good idea.

We need a better city rail system.

WRITING Turn to page 109.

SPEAKING Geography quiz!

1 PAIR WORK What do you know about world geography? Work with a partner and match the places with the superlative phrases. Don't worry if you don't know for sure!

What's the largest island?

Maybe it's ...

The Superlative Earth!

1. Wellington, New Zealand ____
2. Cairo, Egypt ____
3. China ____
4. Russia ____
5. the Pacific ____
6. Angel Falls, Venezuela ____
7. Greenland ____
8. La Paz, Bolivia ____

a. the largest population
b. the biggest ocean
c. the largest island
d. the highest capital city
e. the largest country
f. the most southern capital city
g. the largest city in Africa
h. the highest waterfall

Wellington, New Zealand

Cairo, Egypt

2 GROUP WORK Compare your guesses with other pairs.

We think ... has the largest population in the world.

3 GROUP WORK Think of five superlatives about your city, region, or country. Share your information with your group.

Did you know the oldest restaurant in the country is here?

I didn't know that!

4 OVER TO YOU Choose one of the cities or countries in the geography quiz above and find more information about it. Can you find any green information about the place? Share the information with the class.

GO ONLINE for grammar, vocabulary, and speaking practice

NOW I CAN

SPEAKING	GRAMMAR	LISTENING	READING
☐ describe places.	☐ use superlative adjectives.	☐ understand a geography game show.	☐ understand an article about green places.

05 Where's the party?

SPEAKING
Special cultural events
GRAMMAR
Adverbial clauses: *before*, *after*, and *when*
LISTENING
New Year's traditions
READING
Asian festivals article

WARMUP
What's your favorite celebration?

VOCABULARY

1 **Look at the pictures. Match the pictures with the words. Then write the event(s) under each picture. Listen and check your answers.**

a. bouquet	**e.** fireworks
b. cake	**f.** candles
c. card	**g.** balloons
d. present	**h.** ring

Events	
New Year's	Valentine's Day
Spring Festival	birthday
wedding	

New Year's

____

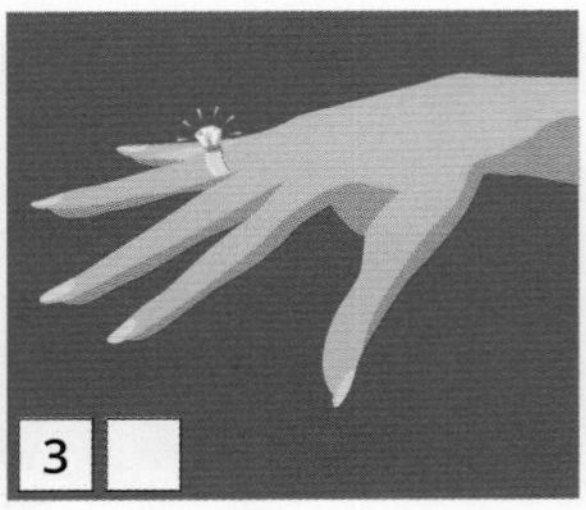

____

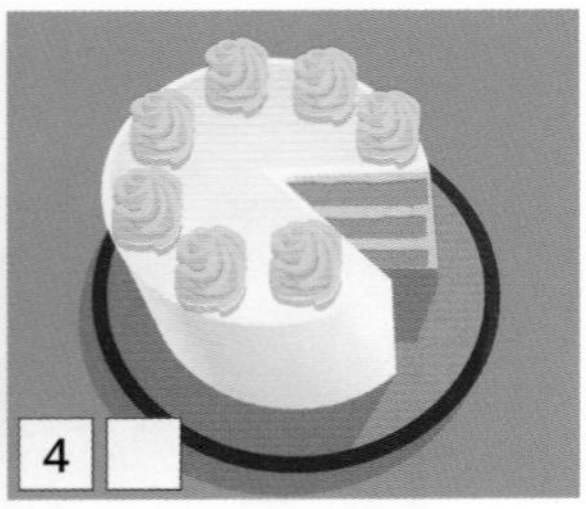

____

____

____

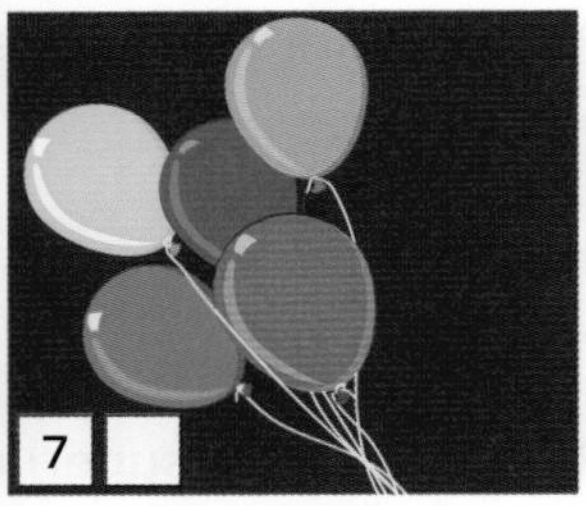

____

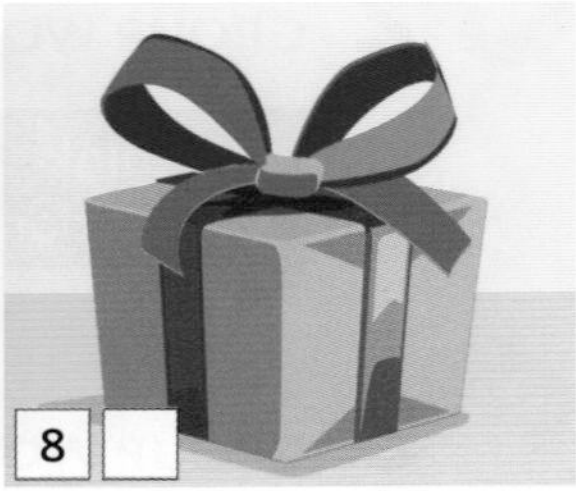

____

2 **Answer the questions.**

1. What was your favorite birthday celebration? __________
2. What do you do for New Year's? __________
3. Is Valentine's Day important in your country? How do people celebrate it?
____
4. Do you like going to parties with fireworks? Why / Why not?
____
5. When do you buy presents for people?
____

3 **PAIR WORK** **Compare your answers with other students. Do you celebrate things in the same way?**

VOCABULARY TIP

Draw pictures to learn new words.

CONVERSATION

I'M GOING
TO A
WEDDING!
1:32

1 **Complete the conversation. Then watch and check your answers. Practice the conversation with a partner.**

a. in a movie theater **b.** Peruvian **c.** Peru **d.** cathedral

Alan	What are you doing this weekend?
Hannah	I'm going to a wedding!
Alan	Nice. Who's getting married?
Hannah	One of my friends. I met her when I was in college. She's from **1** ________ .
Alan	How interesting! I've never been to a **2** ________ wedding.
Hannah	Neither have I. And there's going to be a party before the wedding.
Alan	Really? Isn't the party usually after the wedding?
Hannah	Yes! And it's going to take place **3** ________ .
Alan	What? The party or the wedding?
Hannah	The party!
Alan	What about the wedding?
Hannah	Oh, that's going to be in a **4** ________ .

2 PAIR WORK **Practice the conversation again. Use the ideas below. Add your own ideas.**

1	2	3	4
South Korea	Korean	at a karaoke bar	hotel
Greece	Greek	on a boat	church
________	________	________	________

3 OVER TO YOU **Imagine you're going to a celebration soon. Work in pairs. Make a video of your conversation. Talk about the plans for the celebration.**

Student A	Ask Student B about plans for the weekend. Ask about details.
Student B	Talk about a celebration this weekend. Answer Student A's questions.

LANGUAGE PRACTICE

Adverbial clauses: *before*, *after*, and *when* Grammar Reference page 118

The wedding will be **before** the party begins.
Before the party started, we made a cake.

We usually have a party **when** we graduate from high school.
When she left college, she traveled for a year.

She looked very happy **after** she opened the present.
After the meal is over, we usually go dancing.

SEQUENCE ADVERBS

First, buy a present.
Then get dressed up.
Next, go to the party.
Finally, have fun!

1 Complete the sentences with *before*, *after*, or *when*.

1. When Jacob had a birthday, we gave him a surprise party.
2. ________ he opened the door, we all shouted, "Surprise!"
3. We sang "Happy Birthday" ________ he blew out the candles.
4. ________ he opened his gifts, he sent thank-you cards.

2 Match the information to make complete sentences.

1. When I have a problem, ____
2. I felt really angry ____
3. I try to look good ____
4. Before I went home, ____
5. After I left your party, ____
6. I don't eat breakfast ____

a. after I read her terrible email.
b. when I go to a party.
c. I went to another one!
d. before I come to class.
e. I talk to my best friend.
f. I bought some flowers.

3 PAIR WORK What do you do in these situations? Use sequence adverbs.

1. What do you do when you have a party?
2. What do you do before you go to a party?
3. What do you do when you arrive at a party?
4. What do you do after you get home from a party?

First, I decide who I want to invite. Then I send those people an email. Next, ...

PRONUNCIATION *Intonation of adverbial clauses*

1 Use commas when adverbial clauses are at the beginning of a sentence. Listen. Notice the rising intonation before the comma and the falling intonation at the end of the sentence.

1. **Before I go to a party**, I buy a card.
2. **When I'm tired**, I go to bed early.
3. **When I see friends**, I feel happy.
4. **After I finish work**, I watch TV.

2 Listen again and repeat.

LISTENING

1 BEFORE YOU LISTEN **Look at the photos. How do you think these things are related to New Year's celebrations?**

2 **Listen to people talking about New Year's traditions in their countries. Where do these things happen? Write *I* (Ireland), *K* (Korea), or *B* (Brazil).**

1. People eat seven grapes at midnight. ____
2. People leave the lights on in every room. ____
3. Single people sleep with mistletoe under their pillows. ____
4. People jump over seven waves. ____
5. People clean their houses before the new year. ____

3 **Listen again. Choose (✓) *True* or *False*.**

	True	False
1. In Ireland, it's lucky if a red-haired woman visits you on New Year's Day.	☐	☐
2. People think that Brendan is handsome.	☐	☐
3. In Korea, people usually stay awake on the last night of the year.	☐	☐
4. Korean children often receive money when the new year starts.	☐	☐
5. When the clock strikes midnight, Andrea throws white flowers into the ocean.	☐	☐

4 LISTENING PLUS **Listen to more of the interviews. Complete the chart.**

	Where?	Who with?	What did they do?
Brendan			
Yang-hee			
Andrea			

5 PAIR WORK **Tell your partner about your last New Year's celebration. Ask for more information.**

My family and I went on vacation together.

Where did you go?

SMART TALK ***Dragon boats*** **Student A:** Turn to page 88. **Student B:** Turn to page 100.

READING

1 BEFORE YOU READ **Look at the pictures and scan the article. Which festival do you think seems the most interesting?**

FESTIVAL TIME IN ASIA

PINGXI LANTERN FESTIVAL

The Lantern Festival in Taiwan takes place in February or March, and the most spectacular one is in Pingxi, at the top of a mountain north of Taipei. Thousands of people make lanterns, **make wishes**, and release the lanterns into the night sky.

How did it start?
The inhabitants of Pingxi lit lanterns for friends and family who lived at the bottom of the mountain. The lanterns meant: "Don't worry; we're safe and healthy."

SONGKRAN WATER FESTIVAL

The Songkran Water Festival is the traditional celebration of Thai New Year, and it takes place in April. The best (and longest) Songkran takes place in Chiang Mai. People go into the streets with **buckets** of water, and they also cover their bodies with brightly colored **powder**.

How did it start?
*People visited **monasteries** and gave food to **monks**. They **poured** water over the monks and took some water back to their family and friends. They then poured the water over each other. This brings good luck for the new year.*

BALI KITE FESTIVAL

The Bali Kite Festival takes place every year between July and August. Teams from different villages see who can make the best kites. Sometimes there are teams from other countries. The kites look like birds, fish, or leaves, and are huge—at least four meters wide and ten meters long. In fact, some kites are 100 meters long.

How did it start?
*Farmers wanted to say thank you for good crops and **harvests**.*

2 **Read the article and answer the questions.**

Which festival ...

1. is connected to New Year's celebrations?
2. is connected to farming?
3. involves coloring the skin?
4. is a competition between different villages?
5. has groups working together?
6. takes place first in the year?

3 GROUP WORK **What's your favorite festival? What do you, your friends, or your family do? Tell your group.**

WRITING Turn to page 110.

SPEAKING My favorite months

1 Choose your three favorite months. List the reasons why you like them.

January February March April May June
July August September October November December

Month	Reasons
April	spring, festivals, my birthday
1.	
2.	
3.	

2 CLASS ACTIVITY Find classmates who share at least one of your favorite months. Compare your reasons and write them down.

Why is April one of your favorite months?

Because it's spring. What about you?

Because of spring, but also because it's when I celebrate my birthday!

3 CLASS ACTIVITY Choose one of your favorite months. Tell the class why you and other classmates like it.

Bruno and I like July. He likes it because it's cooler then. I like it because it's our winter break in Brazil.

4 OVER TO YOU Choose a country. Find out about their most important festivals. Share the information with the class.

GO ONLINE for grammar, vocabulary, and speaking practice

NOW I CAN

SPEAKING
- describe special cultural events.

GRAMMAR
- use clauses with *before*, *after*, and *when*.

LISTENING
- understand different New Year's traditions.

READING
- understand an article about Asian festivals.

06 You should try it!

SPEAKING
Suggestions / Obligations

GRAMMAR
should and *have to*

LISTENING
Giving advice

READING
Self-esteem article

WARMUP
Do you think you're a healthy person?

VOCABULARY

1 Look at the pictures. What are the activities? Write the correct letter. Then listen and check your answers.

a. cook healthy food	**c.** get fresh air	**e.** exercise	**g.** talk on the phone a lot
b. get stressed	**d.** eat junk food	**f.** relax	**h.** look at screens too much

2 PAIR WORK Do you do any of the things in the pictures? Tell your partner.

> I exercise twice a week.

> I sometimes eat junk food.

3 PAIR WORK Which of the activities are healthy and which are unhealthy? How often do you do them?

> Getting fresh air is healthy.
> I do that every day.

CONVERSATION

1 Complete the conversation. Then watch and check your answers. Practice the conversation with a partner.

a. good **b.** café **c.** unhealthy

Amy	Hi, Maria. I'm going to the **1** ________ . Do you want to come?
Maria	I can't, because I have to study. I have a math test tomorrow.
Amy	But you're so **2** ________ at math. You should take a break!
Maria	I know I should, but I can't.
Amy	Yes, you can. Come out with me!
Maria	I really should read this book ...
Amy	You shouldn't work so hard. It's **3** ________ . You have to learn how to relax!
Maria	OK.
Amy	Great!
Maria	But I really shouldn't ...

2 PAIR WORK Practice the conversation again. Use the ideas below. Add your own ideas.

1	2	3
movies	great	stressful
park	talented	bad for you
________	________	________

3 OVER TO YOU Work in pairs. Make a video of your conversation. Refuse an invitation with a reason.

Student A	Invite Student B to a place. Persuade him / her to accept the invitation.
Student B	Refuse the invitation and give a reason. Accept the invitation the second time.

CONVERSATION TIP

BEING POLITE

When you refuse an invitation, explain why.

I can't come because I have to study.

LANGUAGE PRACTICE

should* and *have to Grammar Reference page 119

Suggestion	Obligation
What **should** I do?	What **do** I **have to** do?
You **should** try yoga.	You **have to** read these books.
You **shouldn't** eat so much fast food!	You **don't have to** do anything!
Should I drink more water?	What **does** she **have to** do?
Yes, you **should**.	She **has to** study for the math test.
	Do I **have to** pay for the class?
	No, you **don't**.

1 Match the information to make complete sentences.

1. We have to pay the fees __e__
2. Should we warm up ____
3. You should get some fresh air ____
4. You shouldn't exercise ____
5. You don't have to go on a diet ____

a. before we exercise?
b. to lose weight.
c. after a big meal.
d. because you've been indoors all day.
e. before we take the class.

2 Complete the sentences with *should*, *shouldn't*, *have / has to*, or *don't / doesn't have to*.

1. To be healthy, we ______________________ sleep seven or eight hours every night.
2. I have a car, so I ______________________ walk to work. But I still walk for exercise.
3. You ______________________ drink so much soda every day. It's bad for you.
4. We ______________________ pay anything to join the gym. It's free!
5. My sister is really busy. She ______________________ write ten essays before the semester ends.

3 PAIR WORK What should people do to have a healthy lifestyle? List five things. Then discuss your ideas with your partner.

I think people should exercise every day.

Every day? That's too much!

PRONUNCIATION *Reduction of* has to *and* have to

1 Listen. Notice the reduced sound of *to* /tə/ before a consonant sound, or unreduced /tu/ before a vowel sound.

1. He has to eat first. /hæstu ˈit/
2. I have to leave early. /hæftə ˈliv/
3. She has to go now. /hastə ˈgoʊ/
4. They have to pay. /hæftə ˈpeɪ/

2 Listen again and repeat. Try to say the reduced or unreduced sounds.

LISTENING

1 BEFORE YOU LISTEN Look at the activities. How can they keep you healthy?

2 Listen to people talking about their lifestyles. Choose (✓) *True* or *False*.

	True	False
1. Brian works with computers.	☐	☐
2. He walks to work every day.	☐	☐
3. He only eats pizza.	☐	☐
4. Erin doesn't enjoy her work.	☐	☐
5. She does meditation to relax.	☐	☐
6. She usually cooks at home.	☐	☐

3 Listen again and complete the advice. Who is the advice for? Write *B* (Brian), *E* (Erin), or *BO* (both).

1. You ____________ get some exercise. ____
2. You ____________ drive everywhere. ____
3. You ____________ eat so much fast food. ____
4. You ____________ cook fresh food. ____
5. You ____________ drink so much soda. ____

4 LISTENING PLUS Listen to more of Brian and Erin. Choose the correct answer.

1. Erin wants to talk to Brian because ____ .
   a. she thinks she knows him
   b. she saw him earlier
2. Erin is drinking something, and Brian ____ .
   a. wants to try it
   b. doesn't like it
3. Erin and Brian ____ .
   a. both drink a lot of soda
   b. are both drinking coffee
4. Brian's idea of exercise is ____ .
   a. walking to his car
   b. driving to the gym
5. Erin thinks that Brian should ____ .
   a. walk to the gym every day
   b. walk to the gym sometimes
6. Erin and Brian want to ____ .
   a. change their lifestyles
   b. change their lifestyles immediately

5 GROUP WORK What do you do? What should you do? Describe your personal fitness plan and things you should change.

> I drive to school. I should walk and take the bus.

SMART TALK *Help! Is this true?* **Student A:** Turn to page 89.
Student B: Turn to page 101.

READING

1 BEFORE YOU READ **Look at the title. What ideas might be in the action plan?**

Do you have LOW SELF-ESTEEM?

Beat it with this SIX-POINT ACTION PLAN!

1 Make a list of positive things

When you're **feeling low**, you think of bad things: "I'm not good at X. I can't do Y." In fact, we're all good at something, so you should make a list. Add to the list when something good happens or when people say something nice about you. You should keep the list in your pocket and read it every day.

2 ______________________________

Don't spend time with **negative** people. Find **optimistic** people and spend time with them.

3 ______________________________

Doing something new is difficult – this is normal, but try to do something new every month. Join an exercise class, for example. It doesn't matter if you fail. "Try again," said Irish writer Samuel Beckett. "**Fail** again. Fail better."

4 ______________________________

Do you follow famous people on social media? Does it make you sad when you read about their **extraordinary** lives? Stop doing it! Remember – most of the time, they just do **ordinary** stuff.

5 ______________________________

Exercise is good for you, but not if it makes you unhappy. Don't use the treadmill if it makes you feel bad. Try something different: walking, dancing, a yoga class. It's good when you try something new.

6 Remember – you are doing your best!

You should always try to be better, but remember this: nobody's perfect! When you make a mistake, you learn from it.

2 **Read the text. Write the missing subtitles above the correct paragraphs. Which one is not used?**

a. Give yourself a challenge
b. Exercise how you want
c. Take a vacation
d. Hang out with positive people
e. Unfollow celebrities

3 **Read the phrases. What do they mean?**

1. *... so you should make a list.* (par. 1)	What should you make a list of?
2. *... this is normal ...* (par. 3)	What's normal?
3. *Stop doing it!* (par. 4)	What should you stop doing?
4. *... you learn from it.* (par. 6)	What do you learn from?

4 GROUP WORK **Which is the best idea to improve self-esteem? Can you think of any others?**

WRITING Turn to page 110.

SPEAKING *Living a healthy lifestyle*

1 Look at the questions in the *Healthy Living Test*. Add two more questions.

Healthy Living Test

How healthy is your lifestyle?

1	Do you go to bed after midnight?	▢ Yes	▢ No	▢ Sometimes
2	Do you work / study at night?	▢ Yes	▢ No	▢ Sometimes
3	Do you wake up in the morning with a headache?	▢ Yes	▢ No	▢ Sometimes
4	Do you find it hard to concentrate in class?	▢ Yes	▢ No	▢ Sometimes
5	Do you feel tired in the middle of the day?	▢ Yes	▢ No	▢ Sometimes
6	Do you feel sick when you eat certain foods?	▢ Yes	▢ No	▢ Sometimes
7	(your idea) ____________________?	▢ Yes	▢ No	▢ Sometimes
8	(your idea) ____________________?	▢ Yes	▢ No	▢ Sometimes

2 PAIR WORK Ask your partner the questions and select (✓) *yes*, *no*, or *sometimes*. Try to give extra information when you answer.

Do you go to bed after midnight?

Sometimes. I like watching late-night TV!

3 PAIR WORK What do you think your partner can do for a healthier lifestyle? Give your partner advice.

You shouldn't watch TV so much. Maybe you should watch TV only on the weekend.

I'm not sure I can do that!

4 OVER TO YOU Find information about how to avoid or reduce stress. Share the information with the class.

GO ONLINE for grammar, vocabulary, and speaking practice

NOW I CAN

SPEAKING	GRAMMAR	LISTENING	READING
▢ make suggestions and talk about obligations.	▢ use *should* and *have to*.	▢ understand people giving advice.	▢ understand an article about self-esteem.

VIDEO

1 PAIR WORK **Look at the pictures. What do people do to prepare for a wedding? Discuss with your partner.**

CULTURE TIP

The Cocos Islands are a group of 27 coral islands. The population of about 600 lives on only two of the islands, West Island and Home Island.

2 **Watch the video. Number the items in the order they are talked about.**

- [ ] **a.** People who live on the Cocos Islands
- [ ] **b.** The clothes for the wedding
- [ ] **c.** Location of the Cocos Islands
- [ ] **d.** The tents for the wedding
- [ ] **e.** The wedding celebration
- [ ] **f.** Shopping at the supermarket

3 **Watch the video again. Write *T* (true) or *F* (false). Correct the false information.**

1. The Cocos Islands are in the Indian Ocean. ____
2. Three hundred years ago, people from Southeast Asia came to live on the islands. ____
3. Siti's brother is going to get married. ____
4. The supermarket doesn't have any food because the island is very far away. ____
5. The boat arrives with the food the next morning. ____
6. The men and women cook a big meal for the wedding guests ____.
7. Before the wedding, there's a party with dancing and music. ____
8. A Scottish dance is part of the wedding celebration. ____

4 GROUP WORK **Discuss the questions.**

1. Have you ever been to a wedding?
   If **yes**, whose wedding was it? When and where was the wedding? Did you enjoy the wedding? Why / Why not?
   If **no**, imagine your best friend is getting married. What will you wear to the wedding? What present will you give?
2. What are some interesting wedding customs in your country?

READING

1 PAIR WORK **Look at the article. What is it about?**

About | News | Advice

Wedding worries? Jess King can help!

Do you have a question about a wedding?

Click here to send Jess a message now!

I'm messaging from the mall. I just found the most amazing dress to wear to my friend's wedding next week. But it's a white dress. Is that really a big no-no? I thought I should ask you before I buy it.
– Emma, Chicago

Don't buy it! Wearing white to a wedding is one of the worst things you can do! Only the bride should wear white. You should ask the shop assistant if the dress comes in another color. If not, keep looking in other stores.

My girlfriend and I are getting married. Our problem is, we can't agree where to go after the wedding. She thinks the most romantic place to go is a tropical island, to lie on the beach and relax. I don't! That sounds like the most boring vacation ever! I want to do something exciting, like hiking up a volcano or riding a camel in the desert. How can we decide where to go?
– Oliver, Denver

You shouldn't worry too much about where you go. The most important thing is that you're together. And remember, if you go to a tropical island, you don't have to lie on the beach. You could try scuba diving, surfing, or even parasailing. It doesn't have to be boring!

My friends' wedding is next month. They've sent the guests a list with presents they'd like. But even the cheapest item is really expensive! I'm a full-time student and don't have much money. Do you think I have to buy a present, or could I just give them a card?
– Jake, Atlanta

I don't think you should go to the wedding without a present. The best solution may be to buy something with a few friends. If you put in $20 each, you should be able to afford something nice.

2 **Read the article. Complete each sentence with the correct person: *Emma*, *Oliver*, or *Jake*.**

1. ___________ has a question about travel.
2. ___________ has a question about clothes.
3. ___________ doesn't have a job.
4. ___________ isn't sending a message from home.
5. ___________ isn't going to a friend's wedding.

3 PAIR WORK **Do you agree with Jess King's advice? What do you think each person should / shouldn't do?**

Jake shouldn't worry about the wedding present. The most important thing is that he celebrates with his friends.

07 There are too many stores!

SPEAKING
Complaints / Shopping
GRAMMAR
too/not enough; too many/muc
LISTENING
Shopping habits
READING
Unusual shopping mall article

WARMUP
What's your favorite place to shop?

VOCABULARY

1 Look at the pictures. What are the items for sale? Write the correct letter. Then listen and check your answers.

a. accessories b. clothing c. jewelry d. electronics e. shoes

1 b

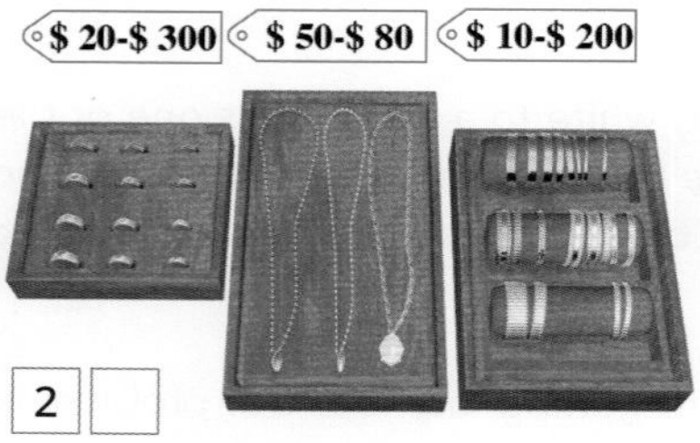

2 ☐

3 ☐

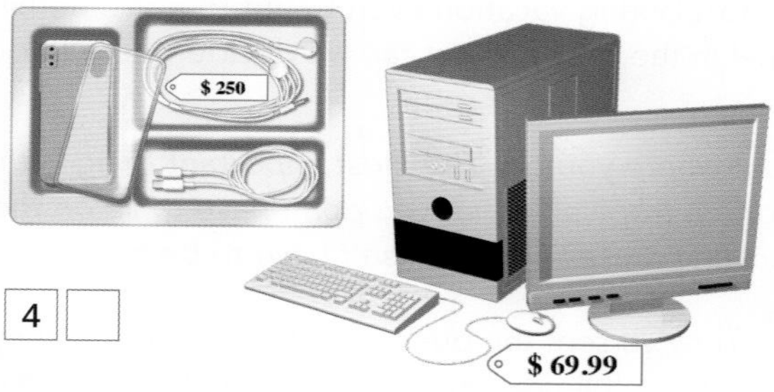

4 ☐

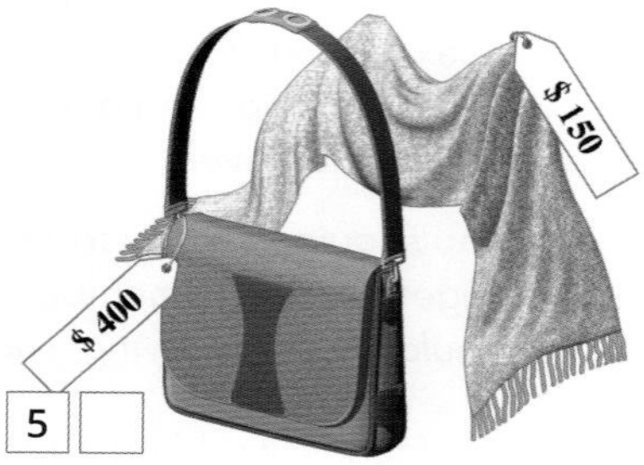

5 ☐

2 PAIR WORK Look at the things to buy above. What do you think about the prices and styles?

Price: expensive / overpriced? reasonable? cheap / inexpensive?

Style: old-fashioned? contemporary? stylish? trendy?

I think those pants are overpriced.

Really? I think they're reasonable. And they're really trendy!

3 PAIR WORK What kind of stores do you like? What kind do you hate?

I love clothing stores.

Really? I hate shopping for clothes!

VOCABULARY TIP

Group new words by theme.

Jewelry
rings,
bracelets
Accessories
scarves, bags

CONVERSATION

IT WAS TOO
EXPENSIVE.
1:32

1 Complete the conversation. Then watch and check your answers. Practice the conversation with a partner.

a. crowded **b.** girlfriend **c.** electronics **d.** laptop

Ricardo	Did you have a good time at the mall?
Patrick	No. There were too many people there.
Ricardo	Right. I was there this morning. It was very **1** ________ .
Patrick	I went to the **2** ________ store, and there weren't enough cashiers. The lines were so long.
Ricardo	Did you buy something there?
Patrick	I bought something for my **3** ________ .
Ricardo	Really? What did you buy?
Patrick	I bought a **4** ________ for her.
Ricardo	Oh, nice!
Patrick	But it was too expensive.
Ricardo	You don't like shopping very much, do you?
Patrick	No, not at all. How did you guess?

2 PAIR WORK Practice the conversation again. Use the ideas below. Add your own ideas.

1	2	3	4
noisy	jewelry	mother	watch
busy	accessories	friend	scarf
________	________	________	________

3 OVER TO YOU Work in pairs. Make a video of your conversation. Ask about a shopping trip where there were problems.

Student A	Ask Student B about a recent shopping trip and what he / she bought.
Student B	Describe the problems. Answer Student A's questions.

LANGUAGE PRACTICE

too / not enough; too many / too much Grammar Reference page 120

Count nouns

There are **too many** people here.

There are**n't enough** cashiers.

Noncount nouns

There's **too much** stuff in my closet!

There is**n't enough** time to go shopping.

Adjectives

This mall is **too** crowded.

These clothes are**n't** trendy **enough**.

1 Complete the sentences with *too*, *too much*, or *too many*.

1. There are _too many_ electronics stores on this street.
2. The clothes are ____________ expensive here. Let's go somewhere else.
3. I can't hear you! The music in this store is ____________ loud!
4. Oh no. I spent ____________ money at the mall today.
5. There are ____________ people in this line. We're going to be here forever!

2 Complete the sentences with *too much*, *too many*, or *not enough*.

1. The lines were long because there were ____________ cashiers.
2. I didn't go to the market, because there was ____________ time.
3. My mother has ____________ credit cards. She has 20!
4. Ugh! There's ____________ noise here. What did you say?
5. This computer has ____________ problems, and it is ____________ fast ____________ .

3 PAIR WORK Complete the conversation with your own ideas. Then practice with a partner.

A I went to ______________________________ yesterday.

B Did you have a good time?

A Yes and no. I bought too many ______________________________ .

B Were there a lot of people there?

A Yes, it was crowded! And there weren't enough ______________________________ .

PRONUNCIATION *Word stress in complaints*

1 Listen. Notice the words that are stressed in complaints.

1. There are too many people here!
2. This place is too noisy!
3. There is not enough time!
4. There is too much stuff here!

2 Listen again and repeat. Be sure to stress the correct words.

LISTENING

1

BEFORE YOU LISTEN Read the comments about shopping at malls and online. Match the words in bold to their definitions. Are the statements true for you?

1. "Online shopping is too **tempting**." ____
2. "There's a great mall near my place. It's very **convenient**." ____
3. "Shopping at a mall is very **stressful**." ____

a. easy to get to
b. worrying
c. attractive

James

Sofia

Gok

2

Listen to the people talking about shopping. Complete the chart.

Who ...	James	Sofia	Gok
1. prefers shopping alone?			
2. prefers shopping at malls?			
3. hates shopping at malls?			
4. enjoys shopping at malls and online?			
5. is worried about shopping online?			

3

Listen again and answer the questions.

1. What doesn't James like about shopping at the mall? ______________________
2. What happened to Sofia's friend? ______________________
3. What does Gok's best friend think about his online shopping habits? ______________________

4

LISTENING PLUS Listen to more of the interviews. Choose (✓) *True* or *False*.

	True	False
1. Gok and Sofia enjoy people-watching at the mall.	☐	☐
2. Sofia doesn't like store assistants talking to her.	☐	☐
3. Gok likes shopping for clothes online.	☐	☐
4. Gok thinks it's a good idea to buy shoes online.	☐	☐
5. Sofia is excited about shopping at the mall with Gok.	☐	☐

SMART TALK *Shopper's paradise?* **Student A:** Turn to page 90.
Student B: Turn to page 102.

READING

1 BEFORE YOU READ **Look at the photo of the shopping mall. What can you see?**

A DIFFERENT KIND OF SHOPPING MALL

The Retuna Shopping Mall, Eskilstuna, Sweden

Eskilstuna is a small riverside town 100 kilometers west of Stockholm, the capital of Sweden. It is where you will find the Retuna Shopping Mall, the world's first mall for secondhand shopping. Everything in the Retuna is **recycled**.

Sweden is good at recycling. It recycles 99% of **household waste**. But Swedish people also buy a lot of new things. "We **consume** too much," said Astrid Karlsson, a visitor at the Retuna, from Stockholm. "My friends and I love shopping, but we want to stop buying things and throwing them away after a short time. This is why I came here."

There are 14 stores at the mall, selling clothes, furniture, bicycles, books, **pottery**, children's toys, and much more. More than 50 people work there. Local people bring their secondhand goods; people check them, **repair** them if necessary, and move them to the shopping stores in the mall. There are nearly 1,000 visitors a day, and after four years, sales were more than three million US dollars.

We need more stores like the ones at the Retuna. At the moment, people recycle less than 1% of their clothes. Most people **throw away** half their clothes after one year, and they go to **landfill sites**.

2 **Read the article. Match the numbers with what they refer to.**

1. four ____
2. 14 ____
3. 50 ____
4. 99 ____
5. 100 ____
6. 1,000 ____

a. the number of people who work at the mall
b. the percentage of household waste that Swedes recycle
c. the number of visitors to the mall every day
d. the number of stores in the mall
e. the number of years the mall has been open
f. the distance in kilometers from the mall to Stockholm

3 **Read the article again. Answer the questions.**

1. What is the Retuna Shopping Mall?
2. Is it in the capital city?
3. What kind of things do the stores sell?
4. What percentage of their clothes do people recycle?

4 GROUP WORK **What do you think about shopping at a mall with only secondhand goods?**

WRITING Turn to page 111.

SPEAKING *A shopping game*

1 PAIR WORK Follow the instructions to play the game.

- Take turns flipping a coin to move on the board. Heads = 1 square. Tails = 2 squares.
- When you land on a square, your partner asks you the question and then a follow-up question for more information.

Do you like shopping at malls?

No, I don't.

Why not?

Because there are too many people.

START

1 Do you like shopping at malls?

2 Where do you usually shop?

3 When do you like to shop?

4 Do you prefer to shop with other people or alone?

5 Have you ever spent too much money shopping?

6 Have you ever had any problems with buying things?

7 What kinds of things do you often buy?

8 What's the worst thing about shopping?

9 How often do you shop online?

FINISH

2 GROUP WORK Now work with another pair. Share the information about your partner. Compare your ideas.

Yuko doesn't like shopping at the mall.

Neither do I. It's too noisy.

Really? I love it! It's always fun.

3 OVER TO YOU Find tips for a good shopping experience. Share them with the class.

GO ONLINE for grammar, vocabulary, and speaking practice

NOW I CAN

SPEAKING	GRAMMAR	LISTENING	READING
☐ make complaints and discuss shopping.	☐ use *too*, *enough*, *many*, *much*.	☐ understand conversations about shopping habits.	☐ understand an article about an unusual shopping mall.

08 Wanted: People who can sing

SPEAKING
Describing preferences
GRAMMAR
Relative clauses
LISTENING
Voicemail messages
READING
Interview tips article

WARMUP
How do your friends describe you?

VOCABULARY

1 **Look at the photos. Complete the captions with five words from the box. Circle the words you don't use. Then listen and check your answers.**

amusing	outgoing	generous	helpful
smart	patient	polite	serious

1 This is my grandma Phyllis. She's always very _generous_ on my birthday!

2 This is my cousin Amy. She's very ____________ .

3 This is my brother Tom. He's the ____________ person in the family.

4 This is my Aunt Alexa. She took me to the airport at 5 a.m.! She's so ____________ .

5 This is my dad, Bob. He never stops telling jokes. People think he's very ____________ .

2 **PAIR WORK** **Use the words above to describe people in your family. Show photos of them if you can. Ask and answer questions about them.**

> This is my cousin Andrea. She's very nice, but she's very serious.

> Can you give me an example?

3 **GROUP WORK** **Use the adjectives above to describe famous people. Do you agree?**

> I think Atsushi Tamura is very funny.

> Do you? I don't think he's funny at all.

CONVERSATION

1 Complete the conversation. Then watch and check your answers. Practice the conversation with a partner.

a. sing		c. children	
b. reliable		d. singing	

Maria What are you doing?
Lily I'm trying to find a summer job.
Maria Oh! How's it going?
Lily Not good. Oh, wait a sec. This looks interesting.
Maria What is it?
Lily It's a company which organizes summer camps. They want people who are good with **1** ____________ .
Maria Well, that's you for sure!
Lily Yes, I guess so. But they also want people who can **2** ____________ .
Maria You can do that!
Lily Well, I had **3** ____________ lessons when I was a kid, but it was a long time ago.
Maria It's like riding a bicycle. You never forget!
Lily It also says they want people who are **4** ____________ . Do you think I am?
Maria Absolutely. More than anyone I know!

2 PAIR WORK Practice the conversation again. Use the ideas below. Add your own ideas.

1	2	3	4
teenagers	paint	art	outgoing
technology	teach martial arts	karate	patient
____________	____________	____________	____________

3 OVER TO YOU Work in pairs. Make a video of your conversation about applying for a vacation job.

Student A Describe a job advertisement and what skills people need.
Student B Ask Student A about the job and say why they can do it. Use positive language.

CONVERSATION TIP

EXPRESSING EMOTION
When you want to support your partner, use positive language and word stress.

Do you think I'm patient?

Abso**lute**ly!

LANGUAGE PRACTICE

Defining relative clauses Grammar Reference page 121

People	Things
Who are you talking to?	**Which** store does he work for?
I'm talking to a guy **who / that** lives in California.	It's a store **which / that** sells electronics.
They want people **who / that** are good with children.	

1 Match the information to make complete sentences.

1. I like having fun, so I prefer people d
2. I'm a quiet person, so I'm looking for a roommate ____
3. I don't like parties, but I went to a reception ____
4. I don't like expensive things, so don't give me gifts ____

a. which was really fun.
b. that cost too much.
c. who doesn't talk too much.
d. that make me laugh.

2 Combine the sentences. Use *who* or *which*.

1. He's a very generous person. He gives his time to everyone.
   He's a very generous person who gives his time to everyone.
2. We met at the new cafe. It has paintings by local artists on the walls.
   ____
3. I interviewed two people for the job. They were very smart.
   ____
4. It's a summer camp. It has classes for very young children.
   ____

3 PAIR WORK Use relative clauses to complete the sentences. Tell your partner. Do you agree?

1. A good friend is someone ...
2. A good teacher is a person ...
3. A good neighbor is someone ...
4. A good boss is someone ...

A good friend is someone who listens.

PRONUNCIATION *Word stress and content words*

1 Listen. Notice the stress on content words.

1. I like movies that are funny.
2. I prefer people who like sports.
3. I'm talking to a guy who works in Florida.
4. My sister works for a store that sells computers.

2 Listen again and repeat. Be sure to stress the correct words.

LISTENING

1 BEFORE YOU LISTEN **Read the message on a house-sitter's website. Find three adjectives that describe a good house-sitter in the text. Then compare with a partner.**

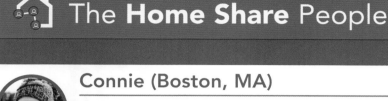

The **Home Share** People

Profile

Connie (Boston, MA)

Hi, my name is Connie, and I'm 20 years old. I'm a business major in Boston, and I'm going to graduate this year. During the summer vacation, I want to travel for a while before I look for a job. I'd like to connect with people who need someone to look after their home and hopefully also animals. I'm an energetic person, as I grew up in a house which was full of animals – cats, dogs, chickens – all kinds! I have an aunt who's a vet, and she taught me a lot, so I'm quite knowledgeable about caring for animals. I'm also very reliable. I have always managed my responsibilities at home and at school well. I like listening to rock music, but I'm not the party type, so your house is safe! Just one thing: I don't have a driver's license, so I need to be in a house that isn't too far from the center of town. Please leave me a message!

2 Listen to three voicemail messages from Anita, Chuck, and Lucy. Which of them refers to the following? Write *A*, *C*, or *L* next to the word or phrase.

1. dogs and cats ____
2. a motorcycle ____
3. a road trip ____
4. cleaning ____
5. horses ____
6. fish ____

3 Listen again and choose (✓) *True* or *False*.

	True	False
1. Anita and her husband are planning to fly across the US.	☐	☐
2. Anita's cleaner is a nice person, but not very reliable.	☐	☐
3. Chuck's house is in the center of a town.	☐	☐
4. Lucy is planning to travel alone.	☐	☐
5. Lucy's house-sitter only has to look after cats and dogs.	☐	☐

4 LISTENING PLUS **Listen to a phone call between Connie and Lucy. Choose the correct answer.**

1. Why is Connie surprised by Lucy's answer about her pets?
   a. Because Lucy doesn't know the name of the dog.
   b. Because Lucy doesn't know how many cats are in the house.
2. Where did most of the cats come from?
   a. From a shopping mall.
   b. From a website.
3. Why does Lucy say the cats are not a problem?
   a. Because they like fish.
   b. Because they sleep most of the time.
4. What information is there to help Connie look after the fish?
   a. There's a website with information.
   b. Lucy is going to write some notes.
5. What does Connie find out about the mall?
   a. You can't take a bus there.
   b. It's further away than she thought.

SMART TALK ***Making connections*** **Student A:** Turn to page 91.
Student B: Turn to page 103.

READING

1 **BEFORE YOU READ** **Where do you think the article is from? Choose the correct answer.**

a. a textbook b. a magazine c. a newspaper

How to **impress** an interviewer

1 First impressions are crucial.

When you meet the person who's going to interview you, look at them, shake hands, and smile. Speak with a clear voice. Also, be on time. Companies like people who are **punctual**. This starts with the interview itself. If you turn up late, don't expect to get a second interview.

2 Do your homework.

Find information about the company that invited you for the interview. Check out its website and look for any news items about it on social media. Practice for the interview—have a friend ask you key questions before the real interview. *Do you work well with other people? Where do you expect to be after five years? Are you* ***ambitious****?*

3 Be energetic and positive, but don't talk too much.

Employers love people who are energetic and **passionate** about something, even if it's just a **pastime**. If you are good at something—chess, running, painting—talk about it. They also want people who are good listeners, so know when to stop talking. Remember—an interview is a dialogue, not a monologue. Also, when the interviewer asks you if you have any questions, **avoid** the obvious ones, and NEVER ask about vacation. Make sure you ask about the company's plans for the future.

4 Bring evidence.

Let's imagine that in your application, you talked about a charity event which you organized. Bring something that shows what you did—a poster, or a news item. Employers are **impressed** by this type of preparation.

2 **Look at the headings in the article and skim the paragraphs. Which suggestion do you think is the most important for an interview?**

3 **Read the article. Complete the sentences with a highlighted word from the text.**

1. The interviewer was very ____________ with her experience.
2. Making a good impression isn't just important, it's ____________ !
3. She answered the question with great enthusiasm because she was very ____________ about the subject.
4. He's very ____________ : he wants to start his own company as soon as possible.
5. He's late again. I can't work with people who aren't ____________ .
6. They want to know about your work experience, so ____________ talking about your favorite TV shows!
7. Watching TV isn't a very interesting ____________ . Think of something more interesting!

4 **GROUP WORK** **Can you think of other important things for an interview? Tell your group.**

I think you should dress professionally.

And comb your hair!

WRITING Turn to page 111.

SPEAKING *The most important thing to me*

1 Look at the list. Add two qualities that are important to you. Then rank them from 1 (most important) to 12 (least important).

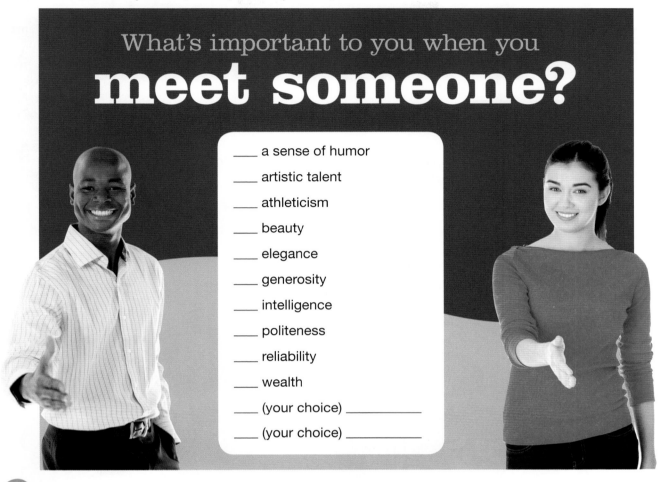

What's important to you when you **meet someone?**

- ____ a sense of humor
- ____ artistic talent
- ____ athleticism
- ____ beauty
- ____ elegance
- ____ generosity
- ____ intelligence
- ____ politeness
- ____ reliability
- ____ wealth
- ____ (your choice) __________
- ____ (your choice) __________

2 PAIR WORK Compare your list with a partner. Explain your reasons.

> I think a sense of humor is the most important thing. I like people who are funny!

> Me too. But I also like people who are smart, so intelligence is the most important to me.

3 GROUP WORK Share your reasons. Try to agree on the five most important qualities.

4 OVER TO YOU Find out about famous couples. How did they meet? What attracted them to each other? Tell the class.

GO ONLINE for grammar, vocabulary, and speaking practice

NOW I CAN

SPEAKING	GRAMMAR	LISTENING	READING
☐ describe my preferences.	☐ use relative clauses for description.	☐ understand voicemail messages about house-sitting.	☐ understand an article about interview tips.

09 What were you doing?

SPEAKING
Narrating past events
GRAMMAR
Past continuous
LISTENING
Describing accidents
READING
Dramatic events article

WARMUP
What do you think is the most dangerous sport?

VOCABULARY

1 Look at the picture. What are the injuries? Write the correct letter. Then listen and check your answers.

a. cut his head	**c.** break his nose	**e.** break an arm	**g.** bruise a leg
b. get a black eye	**d.** lose a tooth	**f.** dislocate a finger	**h.** sprain an ankle

2 **PAIR WORK** Have you or someone you know ever done any of these things? Tell your partner.

Have you ever broken your arm?

No, I haven't, but my brother has.

How did it happen?

He fell off his bicycle.

VOCABULARY TIP

Connect words with people you know. Make sentences.

My brother broke his arm on vacation.

CONVERSATION

WHAT
HAPPENED
TO YOU?
1:32

1 **Complete the conversation. Then watch and check your answers. Practice the conversation with a partner.**

a. soccer **b.** little sister **c.** arm **d.** chair

Adam	Hey, Rosa! What happened to you?
Rosa	I broke my **1** ______ .
Adam	How did you do that?
Rosa	I was watching television, and I fell off my **2** ______ .
Adam	Are you serious?
Rosa	Yes, I am. What about you? Have you ever hurt yourself?
Adam	I've never broken my arm, but I really hurt myself when I was playing **3** ______ once.
Rosa	What happened?
Adam	I crashed into someone and dislocated my shoulder.
Rosa	Oh no! Were you playing for the college team?
Adam	No. I was playing with my **4** ______ in the yard!
Rosa	Was she OK?
Adam	Yes, she was fine. She didn't break anything.

2 **PAIR WORK** **Practice the conversation again. Use the ideas below. Add your own ideas.**

1	2	3	4
shoulder	sofa	football	cousin
finger	bed	basketball	mom
______	______	______	______

3 **OVER TO YOU** **Make a video of your conversation. Talk about an accident or injury you had.**

Student A Ask about Student B's injury. Tell Student B about a similar injury you had.

Student B Tell Student A about your injury and give more details.
Ask and answer questions.

LANGUAGE PRACTICE

The past continuous Grammar Reference page 122

What happened to you?

I **hurt** my knee while I **was jogging** in the park.

While I **was driving** to the hospital, I **had** a car accident.

How did it happen?

I **was playing** soccer when I **ran** into another player.

I **was learning** to windsurf when I **crashed** into someone.

1 Match the information to make complete sentences.

1. I sprained my ankle _e_
2. I was making a sandwich ____
3. She was riding down the street ____
4. My dad tripped over my guitar ____
5. I broke a tooth ____

a. when I cut my finger.
b. while he was cleaning.
c. while I was eating olives.
d. when she fell off her bike.
e. while I was playing soccer.

2 Complete the sentences. Use the simple past or the past continuous form.

1. I ____________ (burn) my fingers while I ____________ (light) the campfire.
2. While he ____________ (run) back home, a dog ____________ (bite) him.
3. We ____________ (cross) the street when the car ____________ (hit) us.
4. My sister ____________ (fall) down the stairs while she ____________ (walk) in her new shoes.

3 PAIR WORK Complete the sentences with information about you. Then talk about it with your partner.

1. I was walking to school when ...
2. I hurt myself while ...
3. I once heard a strange noise while ...
4. While I was waiting for the bus / subway / train, ...

I was walking to school when I fell and broke my wrist.

What did you do?

I called my father, and he took me to the hospital.

USEFUL LANGUAGE

I hurt myself ...
I ran into someone / something.
I crashed into someone / something.
I tripped over someone / something.
I fell off something.
I fell down something.

PRONUNCIATION *Linked sounds with /y/*

1 Listen. Notice how some words or syllables link with a /y/ sound between them.

1. I broke my arm. /maɪˈyɑrm/
2. I was skiing yesterday. /ˈskiyɪŋ/
3. She was playing in the park. /ˈpleɪyɪŋ/
4. I think I sprained my ankle. /maɪˈyæŋkl/

2 Listen again and repeat. Try to link the words or syllables with a /y/ sound.

LISTENING

1 **BEFORE YOU LISTEN** **Look at the photos. What are the people doing? Label each photo with a word from the box.**

canoeing	jet-skiing	waterskiing

A. ____________

B. ____________

C. ____________

2 **Listen to people talking about accidents. Number the pictures above.**

3 **Listen again. Choose the correct answer.**

1. What did Ana do?
   a. She broke her leg. b. She broke her hand. c. She broke her arm.
2. What was she doing when it happened?
   a. She was jet-skiing. b. She was taking a shower. c. She was getting out of the shower.
3. What did Max do?
   a. He cut his hand. b. He broke his arm. c. He sprained his wrist.
4. What was he doing when it happened?
   a. He was driving a car. b. He was cleaning the windows. c. He was relaxing at home.
5. What did Amy do?
   a. She cut her knee. b. She hurt her foot. c. She broke her leg.
6. What was she doing when it happened?
   a. She was walking. b. She was canoeing. c. She was talking to her instructor.

4 **LISTENING PLUS** **Listen to more of Ana, Max, and Amy. Complete the chart.**

	Who are they talking to?	What's the problem now?	What's the other person's advice?
Ana			
Max	*a manager*		
Amy			

SMART TALK ***What happened?*** **Student A:** Turn to page 92.
Student B: Turn to page 104.

READING

1 BEFORE YOU READ Look at the photo. What do you think the story is about?

Home | News | Sports | Weather | Video   Search

Six-year-old boy drives mom's car to school!

When a six-year-old boy from Virginia missed the school bus, he wasn't happy. He always had breakfast at school, and he didn't want to miss it. He had an unusual and **reckless** solution to his problem. He took the keys to his mom's car while she was sleeping and drove her car to school. Well, he almost drove to school.

The boy drove along a highway, across a bridge, and through two **intersections**. He was driving faster than most cars on the road. He was traveling at more than 60 miles (100 kilometers) per hour when he passed some cars on a two-lane road. The other drivers saw the young boy and called the police.

While the police were racing to the **scene**, the boy crashed the car. A tractor drove towards him when he was passing another vehicle. The boy turned quickly, **lost control** of the car, and **smashed** into a pole. He drove 6 miles (10 kilometers) before he crashed.

When the police arrived, the boy was crying, but he was not hurt. He wanted to walk the rest of the way to school, but the police said, "No way!" Instead, they took him to the hospital to check for injuries. He was back at school in the afternoon.

The school principal was happy that the boy was **unharmed**, but she could not understand his actions. "What were you thinking?" she asked him. "I wanted to get to school," the boy replied. "I wanted my breakfast, and I didn't want to miss PE."

The boy isn't very tall. The police think he was probably standing up when he drove the car. In other words, he wasn't wearing a seat belt. He said he knew how to drive the car because he played a lot of video games.

2 Read the article. Put the events in the correct order.

____ a. The police took the boy to the hospital.
____ b. The boy missed his bus to school.
____ c. The boy went to school in the afternoon.
____ d. The boy took his mom's car keys.
____ e. The boy passed some cars.
____ f. The boy crashed the car.

3 Read the article again. Choose (✓) *True* or *False*.

	True	False
1. The boy's mom knew he was driving the car.	☐	☐
2. The boy likes having breakfast at school.	☐	☐
3. When the police found the boy, he was happy.	☐	☐
4. He was wearing a seat belt while he was driving.	☐	☐
5. The boy's parents taught him to drive a car.	☐	☐

4 PAIR WORK Close your books. Take turns telling the story in your own words.

The story is about a six-year-old boy who drove his mom's car ...

WRITING Turn to page 112.

SPEAKING Have you ever ... ?

1 Choose one of the questions (A–D). Read the follow-up questions and think about your answers to them.

A. Have you ever seen or met a famous person?
Who was the person?
Where were you?
What were you doing?
What did you do? Did you say anything?

B. Have you ever seen an accident?
Where did it happen?
Why were you there?
What were you doing?
What happened next?

C. Have you ever witnessed a crime?
When did it happen?
What were you doing?
What did you see?
What happened next?

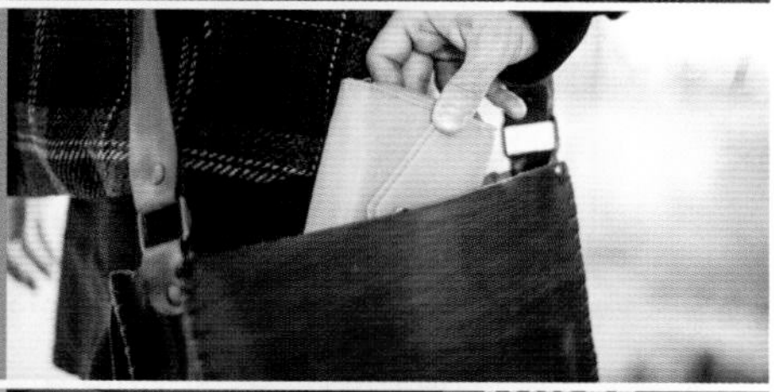

D. Have you ever performed in front of an audience?
Where were you?
What did you perform?
What was the reaction of the audience?
How did you feel before and after the performance?

2 **GROUP WORK** Tell the other students what happened to you. Answer their questions asking for more details.

> I saw Neymar in a coffee shop. I was having coffee when he walked in.

3 **CLASS ACTIVITY** Tell the class what happened to someone in your group.

> Maria saw Neymar in a coffee shop! She was ...

4 **OVER TO YOU** Choose an interesting recent news story and find out more about it. Share the information with the class.

GO ONLINE for grammar, vocabulary, and speaking practice

NOW I CAN

SPEAKING	GRAMMAR	LISTENING	READING
☐ narrate past events.	☐ use the past continuous.	☐ understand descriptions of accidents.	☐ understand an article about a dramatic event.

BONUS Units 7–9

VIDEO

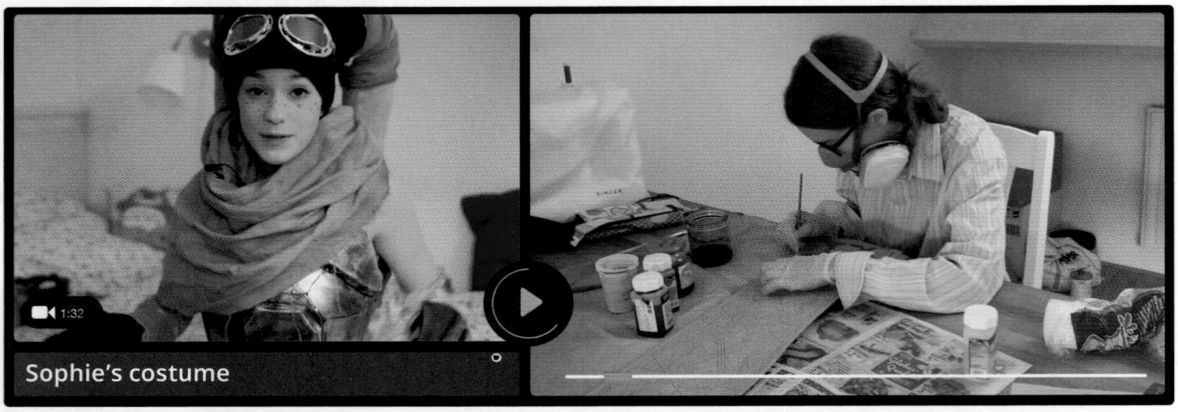

1 PAIR WORK Look at the pictures. What kind of person do you think Sophie is? Discuss your answer with your partner.

2 Watch the video. What is it about? Choose the best answer.

a. The mistakes Sophie made while she was making a costume

b. What Sophie learned from the experience of making a costume

c. Why Sophie loves dressing up in costumes

CULTURE TIP

The term *cosplay*, short for *costume play*, was first used in Japan in 1984. A *cosplayer* is someone who dresses up in a costume to look like a fictional character.

3 Watch the video again. Choose the correct option to complete the statements.

1. Sophie's cosplay costume is a character from ____ .
   a. Comic Con **b.** Germany **c.** Star Wars
2. It took Sophie about ____ to design and make the costume.
   a. a week **b.** two weeks **c.** three weeks
3. Sophie loves cosplay because she enjoys ____ .
   a. learning new skills **b.** buying new clothes **c.** making new friends
4. If something doesn't work the first time, you need to be ____ .
   a. awesome **b.** talented **c.** patient
5. Sophie's birthday is in ____ .
   a. January **b.** June **c.** July
6. Sophie made a video when she went to ____ .
   a. Comic Con **b.** CosDay **c.** Gamescom
7. Sophie thinks cosplay is a good way to find people who have the same ____ as her.
   a. interests **b.** sense of humor **c.** skills

4 GROUP WORK Answer the questions about a skill you have learned. Tell your group.

- What is the skill?
- When did you learn it?
- Why did you learn it?
- Was it easy or difficult? Why?

> I've always thought surfing is an exciting sport, so last summer I decided to take lessons. At first, it was really difficult because I fell off the board a lot. But after a week, it was much easier.

READING

1 PAIR WORK **Look at the picture and the title. What do you think the story is about?**

Not such a fun run!

by Harry Miller

Last month, I was walking home from campus when I saw my friend, Mia. I've known Mia since elementary school, and she's the most generous person I know. So, I wasn't surprised to hear she was organizing a charity event. She explained it was a five-kilometer run to raise money for a charity which helps sick animals.

Athleticism is not one of my qualities. I am, however, passionate about animal welfare, so I agreed to take part. Then, Mia told me all the runners had to wear an animal costume! I'm someone who hates dressing up, but it was too late to change my mind.

I didn't have enough time to make a costume, so I decided to rent one. I went to a costume store downtown and looked around, but I wasn't having too much success. The rabbit costume was too big, the dog costume wasn't big enough, the camel one looked too uncomfortable, and the lion costume was really overpriced. I was starting to feel disappointed when a helpful sales assistant found the perfect costume. A panda! I've always loved pandas, and this costume was the right size and a reasonable price.

On the morning of the run, I was feeling excited at the starting line. Around me, there were runners dressed as all kinds of animals. Finally, someone shouted, "three, two, one, GO" and the race began. Everything was going well until suddenly, the monkey and zebra in front of me ran into each other and fell over. I tripped over them, and the two goldfish behind us fell on top of me. Fortunately, there were no serious injuries – no broken or dislocated bones and no lost teeth. Just a sprained ankle, some cuts and bruises, and two black eyes … on my panda costume.

2 **Read the story and answer the *yes/no* questions. Give more information.**

1. Did Harry and Mia first meet each other on campus?
2. Does Harry like wearing costumes?
3. Was Harry too busy to make a costume?
4. Did Harry rent a panda costume?
5. Was Harry the first runner to fall over?
6. Did any of the runners break a bone?

3 PAIR WORK **Ask and answer the questions. Give more information.**

1. Have you ever organized or taken part in a charity event?
2. Have you ever worn a costume?
3. Have you ever fallen over while you were running?

10 I used to sing.

SPEAKING
Past habits
GRAMMAR
used to
LISTENING
Family histories
READING
Biographical article

WARMUP
What was your favorite year at school?

VOCABULARY

1 Which of these schools did you go to?

elementary school	primary school	middle school
junior high school	high school	summer school

2 Look at the photos. What are the school activities and clubs? Write the correct letter. Then listen and check your answers.

a. choir **b.** athletics **c.** orchestra **d.** math club **e.** drama club **f.** science club

3 **PAIR WORK** Ask and answer questions about school activities and clubs.

What extra activities did you do in junior high?

I was in the drama club.

Did you act in any plays?

Yes! I was in *Hamlet*!

CONVERSATION

1 **Complete the conversation. Then watch and check your answers. Practice the conversation with a partner.**

a. play **b.** musician **c.** playing **d.** in an orchestra

Maria	Ricardo, you're a really good **1** ______________ !
Ricardo	Thank you!
Maria	Do you **2** ______________ a lot?
Ricardo	Not anymore. I used to ______________ when I was younger.
Maria	Really?
Ricardo	Yeah, I used to be **3** ______________ when I was at school.
Maria	Really? Was it good?
Ricardo	Good? It was excellent! We used to win competitions!
Maria	So, why did you stop **4** ______________ ?
Ricardo	I don't know. I guess I wanted to try different things.
Maria	Well, I think you should start again. You're very good!

2 PAIR WORK **Practice the conversation again. Use the ideas below. Add your own ideas.**

1	2	3	4
singer	sing	in a choir	singing
actor	act	in a drama club	acting
______	______	______	______

3 OVER TO YOU **Work in pairs. Make a video of your conversation. Talk about school activities when you were younger.**

Student A	Ask Student B about a school activity or club. Show interest by asking for more details.
Student B	Give details and confirm or correct your partner by repeating part of his / her question.

CONVERSATION TIP

CHECKING AND CONFIRMING

Repeat part of your partner's question to confirm or correct information.

Was it good?

Good? It was excellent!

LANGUAGE PRACTICE

used to Grammar Reference page 123

I **used to** be in the drama club, and my brother **used to** be in the orchestra.
I **never used to** like classical music, but now I love it!
I **didn't use to** play soccer when I was younger. I started in college.
Did you **use to** sing when you were younger?
Yes, I **did**. I **used to** be in a choir.
No, I **didn't**. I **didn't use to** sing, but I **used to** dance!

1 **Complete the conversations with the correct form of *used to* and the correct verb from the box. You will use some of the verbs more than once.**

do have play sing spend

1. A Did you ___use to play___ soccer when you were in high school?
   B No, my school ________ a soccer team. Now it does.
   A So, what did you ________?
   B Video games. I ________ all my time on the computer.
2. A Your brother is really good at ping pong! Did he ________ when he was a child?
   B No, he ________ any sports.
   A What did he ________ in his free time?
   B He ________ in the school choir.

2 PAIR WORK **Complete the sentences with information about you. Compare your answers. Ask for more information.**

1. When I was in elementary school, I used to … .
2. After school, my friends and I used to … .
3. When I was younger, I didn't use to … , but now I do.
4. I never used to like … , but now I … .

When I was in elementary school, I used to draw a lot.

Me too. What did you use to draw?

PRONUNCIATION *Linking and vowel reduction in* used to

1 **Listen. Notice how the *d* links to the *t*, and how the *o* sound changes when *to* links to a consonant.**

used to sing /ˈyust tu sɪŋ/	**used to sing** (linked) /ˈyus tə sɪŋ/
1. He used to **s**ing well.	He /ˈyus tə sɪŋ/ well.
2. She used to **b**e a teacher.	She /ˈyus tə bi/ a teacher.
3. Mark used to **e**xercise every day.	Mark /ˈyus tu eksərsaɪz/ every day.
4. I used to **w**atch cartoons.	I /ˈyus tə wɒtʃ/ cartoons.

2 **Listen again and repeat. Try to say the reduced sound.**

LISTENING

1 BEFORE YOU LISTEN **Look at these free-time activities. Do you do any of them? Did your parents or grandparents use to do them?**

collecting stamps

climbing trees

making models

2 **Listen to Carl interview his father and his grandfather Giorgio. Answer the questions.**

1. Where were Carl's father and grandfather born? ______________________________
2. How long have they lived in the US? ______________________________
3. How old are they now? ______________________________

3 **Listen again. Choose the correct answer.**

1. Where did the Rossi family live when they first came to the US?
   a. New York City **b.** New Jersey **c.** California
2. What did Carl's father use to do when he was little?
   a. watch cartoons on his phone **b.** watch TV **c.** play computer games
3. Where did Carl's father use to go when he was a teenager?
   a. to the beach **b.** to the mall **c.** to the movies
4. What did Carl's grandfather Giorgio use to do when he was a kid?
   a. play soccer at the beach **b.** go for long walks **c.** go to the mall
5. What was one of Carl's grandfather's favorite activities?
   a. making model airplanes **b.** collecting stamps **c.** climbing trees

4 LISTENING PLUS **Listen to Carl interview his grandmother Silvana. Write *T* (true) or *F* (false). Correct the false statements.**

1. Carl's grandparents met at school. ____
2. Silvana used to walk to school with Giorgio. ____
3. All the children in the village went to the same school. ____
4. Silvana was an only child. ____
5. Silvana left school earlier than the other girls. ____
6. Silvana's brothers didn't help with housework. ____

SMART TALK *Before they were famous*

Student A: Turn to page 93.
Student B: Turn to page 105.

READING

1 BEFORE YOU READ **What do you know about Lady Gaga? Share your information with the rest of the class.**

Home | News | Sports | Weather | Entertainment | Search

You probably know her real name is Stefani Germanotta. Now here are ...

Ten things you didn't know about Lady Gaga

1. "Radio Ga Ga" is a song by British band Queen, and it was the **inspiration** for her stage name.
2. She started playing the piano when she was four years old. Before she could play, she used to sit at the piano for an hour a day.
3. Her **ancestors** were Italian and French Canadian.
4. She attended the oldest **private** girls' school in Manhattan. After school, she used to work as a waitress in a diner. She was the only student at the school with an after-school job.
5. When she was in college, someone created a Facebook group called "Stefani Germanotta, you will never be famous."
6. She donated all the **proceeds** from her show at New York's Radio City Music Hall in January 2010 to help people after an earthquake in Haiti. The total was more than $500,000.
7. In September 2017, she had to **cancel** a concert in Montreal, Canada, because she had a cold. She bought $1,000 worth of pizza for disappointed fans outside her hotel.
8. She appeared in the movie *A Star Is Born* in 2018. It was one of the most successful musicals in movie history. It cost $36 million and made more than $430 million at the **box office**.
9. There is a course at the University of South Carolina named "Lady Gaga and the Sociology of Fame." Students study the importance of her music, music videos, and her clothes and makeup.
10. She likes drinking tea and always takes a purple cup and **saucer** with her when she goes on tour.

2 Read the article. Answer the questions.

1. Where did she get her stage name?
2. What did she use to do after school?
3. What did she give money to after a show in 2010?
4. Why did she cancel a concert in Montreal, and what did she do for her fans?
5. What does she always take on tour?

3 GROUP WORK **Answer the questions and give details.**

When you were in middle or high school, did you use to:

- go to live concerts?
- have a part-time job?
- play a musical instrument or sing in a choir?

I never used to go to live concerts.

Really? I used to go to live concerts all the time. I saw ...

WRITING Turn to page 112.

SPEAKING *Find someone who used to …*

1 Look at the questions in the survey. Add one more activity to each list.

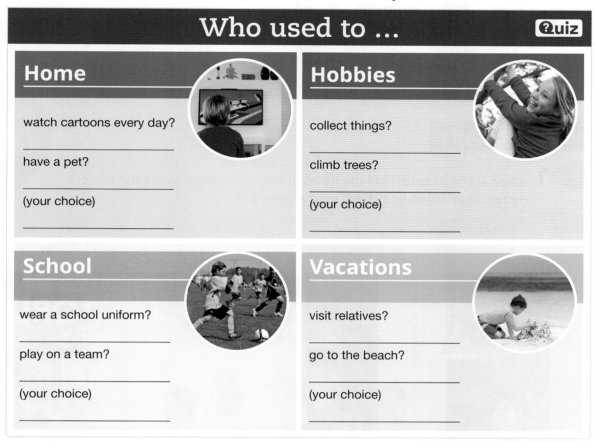

Who used to … Quiz

Home

watch cartoons every day?

____

have a pet?

____

(your choice)

____

Hobbies

collect things?

____

climb trees?

____

(your choice)

____

School

wear a school uniform?

____

play on a team?

____

(your choice)

____

Vacations

visit relatives?

____

go to the beach?

____

(your choice)

____

2 CLASS ACTIVITY Find classmates who used to do the activities. Try to get extra information.

Did you use to collect things?

Yes, I did.

What did you use to collect?

3 GROUP WORK Who used to do the most interesting things? Tell your group. Comment on the information.

Daniel used to have a pet snake. I think that's cool!

Wow, a snake? That's dangerous!

4 OVER TO YOU Choose a movie star. Find out what he / she used to do when he / she was younger. Tell the class.

GO ONLINE for grammar, vocabulary, and speaking practice

NOW I CAN

SPEAKING

- ☐ talk about past habits.

GRAMMAR

- ☐ use *used to*.

LISTENING

- ☐ understand family histories.

READING

- ☐ understand a short biography about a famous person.

11 You'll save money if ...

SPEAKING
Speculating
GRAMMAR
Zero and first conditionals
LISTENING
Single-use plastics
READING
News articles about the environment

WARMUP
What plastic things did you use today?

VOCABULARY

1 Look at the picture. Find the items in the coffee shop. Write the correct letter. Then listen and check your answers.

a. plastic cups	c. plastic spoons	e. reusable cup	g. plastic water bottle
b. plastic bag	d. plastic straws	f. reusable bag	h. cardboard tray

2 GROUP WORK How "green" are you? Discuss the questions.

1. Do you use plastic cups in coffee shops or takeout restaurants?
2. Do you buy water in plastic bottles?
3. Do you take reusable bags to stores, or use plastic bags?
4. What things do you recycle at home, school, or work?

Do you use plastic cups in coffee shops?

No, I take a reusable cup.

VOCABULARY TIP

List words that go together to learn new vocabulary.

Plastic—spoons, bottles, straws

Reusable—cups, bags

CONVERSATION

THINGS
MIGHT GET
BETTER!
1:32

1 Complete the conversation. Then watch and check your answers. Practice the conversation with a partner.

a. barista b. spoon c. coffee d. a hundred

Lily	Hi. Is it OK if I have my **1** ________ in my own cup?
Carlos	Oh, don't worry about it. I have these plastic ones.
Lily	Sorry, I do worry about it. If you use plastic cups, you make more waste.
Carlos	Oh, come on! I only use about **2** ________ cups a day.
Lily	If people bring their own cups, you won't have to use any.
Carlos	OK, give me your cup. I'll put the ________ in it.
Lily	Thank you.
Carlos	Here you go.
Lily	I don't need this **3** ________, thank you.
Carlos	It's OK. It isn't a problem. They're very cheap.
Lily	Maybe it isn't a problem. But you'll save money if you stop using them.
Carlos	OK, OK, I'll stop using them.
Lily	Thank you. If every **4** ________ does the same, things might get better!

2 PAIR WORK Practice the conversation again. Use the ideas below. Add your own ideas.

1	2	3	4
tea	two hundred	napkin	coffee shop
soup	three hundred	cardboard tray	restaurant
________	________	________	________

3 OVER TO YOU Work in pairs. Make a video of your conversation. Order something from your partner.

Student A Order something from Student B in a store. Refuse to use a plastic bag and give Student B a reason to change.

Student B Give Student A what he / she orders. Apologize for using a plastic bag.

LANGUAGE PRACTICE

Zero and first conditionals Grammar Reference page 124

Zero conditional

If you use plastic cups, **you make** more waste.

If you don't use plastic cups, **you don't make** any waste.

First conditional

If you stop using plastic cups, **you'll save** money.

If people bring their own cups, **you won't have to** use any.

If* clauses with *may* or *might

If every barista does the same as you, **things may / might get** better!

If we don't stop putting garbage in the ocean, **the fish may / might not survive.**

you will → you'll

you will not → you won't

1 Match the information to make sentences.

1. If we use plastic items only once, _d_
2. If more people take the bus, ____
3. If you pay your bills online, ____
4. If plastic bags go into the ocean, ____

a. it saves paper.
b. fish eat them.
c. it reduces air pollution.
d. we create a lot of waste.

2 *Will* or *won't*? Complete the sentences using *will* or *won't* and a verb from the box.

buy catch get need

1. If you don't leave now, you ____________ your train.
2. If you take your own bag, you ____________ to use a plastic one at the store.
3. If we don't change our habits, the situation ____________ worse.
4. If they stop using plastic cups, I ____________ my coffee there. I want to support companies that care about the environment.

3 Complete the sentences with the simple present or *will / may / might* and the base form of the verbs in parentheses.

1. If we __________ people to bring their own cups, I think they __________ . (ask, agree)
2. We don't know. If we __________ to use plastic bags, we __________ the oceans. (continue, destroy)
3. Things __________ only __________ if the owners of coffee shops __________ to change. (improve, agree)
4. If we __________ something, the human race ____________ . (not do, not survive)

PRONUNCIATION *Word stress in conditional sentences*

1 Listen to the conditional sentences and underline the stressed words or syllables.

If we don't stop putting garbage in the ocean, the fish might not survive.

1. If you don't take an umbrella, you'll get wet.
2. If class starts on time, we'll miss the beginning.
3. You'll catch the bus if you leave now.
4. I might see my sister if I go home tomorrow.

2 Listen again and repeat the examples.

LISTENING

1 **BEFORE YOU LISTEN** **You are going to listen to an interview about plastic. Match the phrases to their correct definitions. Which phrase refers to something green?**

a. plastic waste   b. single-use plastic
c. recyclable plastic

1. __________: something made of plastic that you throw away after using it once
2. __________: trash made out of plastic objects
3. __________: a type of plastic that can be transformed into another type of plastic or material

2 **Now listen to the interview and correct the statements.**

1. People are creating small hills of garbage. __________
2. If you eat fish, you probably don't eat plastic. __________
3. There will be eight million metric tons of plastic in our oceans by 2050. __________
4. In the US, people buy 1,000 plastic water bottles every minute. __________
5. Plastic is useless, and the biggest problem is single-use plastic. __________
6. The average American uses more than 500 sandwich bags a week. __________

3 **Listen again and complete the two sections of the interview.**

1. **Interviewer** So, first of all, Doctor White: single-use plastics. What's the [1]__________ ?
Doctor White The [2]__________ is very [3]__________ . People use too much [4]__________ and throw it away. They don't [5]__________ enough.

2. **Interviewer** So what [6]__________ do you want to give the listeners tonight?
Doctor White The [7]__________ is [8]__________ : if we continue to [9]__________ single-use plastic items, we will have mountains of plastic garbage [10]__________ , but most importantly in the [11]__________ .

4 **LISTENING PLUS** **Now listen to the second part of the program. Which of the items does Doctor White talk about?**

☐ reusable shopping bags
☐ metal knives and forks
☐ reusable water bottles
☐ stainless steel straws
☐ reusable sandwich bags

5 **GROUP WORK** **What examples of recycling are there in your neighborhood, town, or city?**

In our neighborhood, there are places to recycle glass and plastic.

I live near a recycling center where you can take anything—furniture, clothes, bottles.

SMART TALK ***Making houses from plastic bottles***

Student A: Turn to page 94.
Student B: Turn to page 106.

READING

1 BEFORE YOU READ **Look at the photos and predict what the texts are about.**

And now the good news!

1 THE #TRASHTAG CHALLENGE

The #trashtag **challenge** aims to **persuade** people to clean up their local area. This is what you do:

- find an area with a lot of garbage
- take a photo
- clean up the garbage
- **sort** it and recycle anything you can
- take another photo
- post the two photos online
- ask friends to take the challenge

If someone asks you, you have to do it!

2 STOP GLOBAL WARMING: PLANT TREES!

Trees are important—they provide a home for some animals, clean the air, and produce oxygen. Now the planet needs more trees, but where do we start? **Researchers** at a university in Switzerland made a map of the best places on the planet to plant new trees—areas where there are no people. They found a lot of land, **mainly** in six countries: Russia, the US, Canada, Australia, Brazil, and China. If we plant trees in those areas, the air in the **whole** world will be cleaner.

2 **Read the texts and answer the questions.**

1. How many photos do you take in the #trashtag challenge?
2. What do you do after you post the photos?
3. What do you do if someone asks you to take the #trashtag challenge?
4. Why are trees important?
5. What is important when we choose places for new trees?

3 GROUP WORK **Do you know any other good news about the environment? Tell the group and give details if you can. Use the topics below or your own ideas.**

- green ideas in stores and cafes
- green spaces and parks
- solar panels

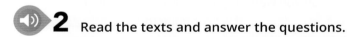

Our local supermarket stopped using plastic bags.

WRITING Turn to page 113.

SPEAKING How green are you?

1 PAIR WORK **Answer the questions in the questionnaire. Then compare your answers.**

How green are you? Quiz

1 How do you usually come to class?
a. I walk.
b. I come by car / taxi.
c. I come by bicycle.
d. I come by public transportation.

2 How often do you use public transportation?
a. always
b. sometimes
c. never
d. never (because I walk or cycle everywhere)

3 Do you drive a car?
a. Yes, very often.
b. Yes, but not very often.
c. I have a driver's license, but I don't drive.
d. I don't have a driver's license.

4 How often do you buy new clothes?
a. every week
b. every month
c. maybe once a year
d. I never buy new clothes.

5 What do you do with your old clothes?
a. I throw them away.
b. I give them to someone in my family.
c. I take them to a recycling center.
d. I give them to charity.

6 Do you buy water in plastic bottles?
a. always
b. often
c. sometimes
d. never

7 What do you do with plastic waste?
a. I throw it away.
b. I try to use it again.
c. I take it to a recycling center.
d. I don't buy stuff if it's made of plastic.

8 Do you buy food from fast-food or takeout restaurants?
a. Yes, every day.
b. Yes, very often.
c. Yes, but not very often.
d. No, never.

9 Where do you get fresh food?
a. from a supermarket
b. from a local store
c. from a farm or local garden
d. I never buy fresh food.

10 How did you travel on your last vacation?
a. by car
b. by plane
c. by ship / train
d. by bus

2 GROUP WORK **Are there any problems about being green in your town or city?**

I want to recycle old clothes, but there isn't a clothes recycling center in my town.

3 OVER TO YOU **Find out about a green project in your town or city. Share the information with the class.**

GO ONLINE for grammar, vocabulary, and speaking practice

NOW I CAN

SPEAKING	GRAMMAR	LISTENING	READING
☐ make speculations.	☐ use the zero and first conditionals	☐ understand someone talking about single-use plastics.	☐ understand an article about the environment.

12 You could be a lifeguard.

SPEAKING
Future plans
GRAMMAR
Modals for possibility, speculation, and deduction
LISTENING
Careers and studying abroad
READING
Volunteering on vacation

WARMUP
Have you ever had a summer job?

VOCABULARY

1 Look at the picture. Find the occupations. Write the correct letter. Then listen and check your answers.

a. sales clerk	**c.** tour guide	**e.** doorman	**g.** receptionist
b. lifeguard	**d.** server	**f.** bus driver	**h.** park ranger

2 **PAIR WORK** Ask and answer questions about the occupations.

Have you ever worked as a hotel receptionist?

No, but I've worked as a doorman. Would you like to be a receptionist?

3 **CLASS ACTIVITY** What are the good things about working in a hotel? What are the difficult things?

Good things: you meet people from all over the world.

Difficult things: you have to work long hours!

CONVERSATION

1 **Complete the conversation. Then watch and check your answers. Practice the conversation with a partner.**

a. a lifeguard **b.** a pool **c.** good at swimming **d.** a coffee

Amy	Hi, Adam. Do you want to go for **1** ______ ?
Adam	I can't. I'm looking for a summer job. I need a job to pay my rent.
Amy	Oh, poor you. You must be very worried.
Adam	You're right. I am.
Amy	What kind of thing do you want to do?
Adam	Well, that's the problem—I have no idea.
Amy	Well, you're **2** ______ . You could get a job as **3** ______ .
Adam	Where could I do that?
Amy	You could do it in **4** ______ downtown.
Adam	That's true.
Amy	You never know. You might want to do it for the rest of your life!

2 **PAIR WORK** **Practice the conversation again. Use the ideas below. Add your own ideas.**

1	2	3	4
a walk	good at languages	a hotel receptionist	a hotel
a run	good with people	a tour guide	a travel agency
______	______	______	______

3 **OVER TO YOU** **Work in pairs. Make a video of your conversation. Talk about applying for a job.**

Student A Invite Student B somewhere. Show you understand how he / she feels. Make suggestions for possible jobs.

Student B Explain you can't go with Student A because you need money and are looking for a job. Ask Student A for suggestions about what you could do.

CONVERSATION TIP

EXPRESSING EMOTION

Show you understand how someone feels.

You must be very worried.

LANGUAGE PRACTICE

Modals for possibility, speculation, and deduction Grammar Reference page 125

Possibilities

You **could get** a job as a lifeguard.

It **might be** fun.

I **may teach** swimming.

Speculation

You **must be** very worried.

You **may / might want** to do it for the rest of your life.

Deductions

It **must be** the mailman.

It **can't be** the mailman. He's already been here.

The lights are off. They **must not be** at home.

I just met them downtown. They **can't be** at home.

1 Read the example. Then suggest possible jobs for the other people.

1. He's good at swimming. He could get a job as a lifeguard.
2. She's good at languages. ____________________
3. He's good at cooking. ____________________
4. She's a good driver. ____________________
5. He loves nature and taking people on tours. ____________________

2 Complete the conversations with *must be*, *might be*, or *can't be*.

1. **A** I think she's at the concert.
   B She __________ —she doesn't have a ticket.
2. **A** Who's at the door?
   B It __________ Alex. He always comes at this time.
3. **A** It's 11 p.m.! Is someone in the kitchen?
   B I don't know. It __________ Helen. She likes cooking late.
4. **A** Do you think he's our new teacher?
   B He __________ our new teacher. Our new teacher is a woman.

3 PAIR WORK Take turns responding to the sentences using *can't be*.

1. It must be after midnight.
2. Is that man the bus driver?
3. I think that woman is a student.
4. I think he's working as a lifeguard.

It must be after midnight.

It can't be after midnight. The stores are still open!

PRONUNCIATION *Reduction of* must / can't / might be

1 Listen. Notice the reduced *t* in *must be*, *can't be*, and *might be*. Then listen again and repeat.

	Unreduced	Reduced
1. You **must be** very worried.	/ˈmʌst bi/	/ˈməs bi/
2. She **can't be** the teacher.	/ˈkænt bi/	/ˈkæm bi/
3. There **might be** a good reason.	/ˈmaɪt bi/	/ˈmaɪ bi/

LISTENING

1 BEFORE YOU LISTEN **Look at the careers. Do you think they're interesting? Why or why not?**

space engineering

audio production

fashion design

2 **Listen to students on a radio show. Complete the chart with what they are studying now and where they may study in the future.**

	Name	is studying ...	may study in ...
1.	Jim		
2.	Megan		
3.	Richard		

3 **Listen again. Choose (✓) *True* or *False*.**

	True	False
1. Jim is interested in one country with space programs.	☐	☐
2. Jim plans to go to Russia if he gets a visa.	☐	☐
3. Megan wants to do a course in Europe.	☐	☐
4. Megan thinks London is a good place to go because it isn't an expensive city.	☐	☐
5. Richard's mother has contacts in fashion houses in Milan and Paris.	☐	☐
6. If Richard doesn't get a job in Milan, he will go to Paris.	☐	☐

4 LISTENING PLUS **Listen to more of the radio show. Answer the questions.**

1. Where does Nancy live and what is she studying? ____________________

2. Who organized her visit to China? ____________________

3. What and where did Sam study? ____________________

4. What is good about the place? ____________________

5. Where does Anita work? ____________________

6. Why does she suggest going to Japan? ____________________

SMART TALK *What are your plans?* **Student A:** Turn to page 95.
Student B: Turn to page 107.

READING

1 BEFORE YOU READ **What do you know about sharks and giant tortoises?**

A volunteer vacation

It's almost vacation time. You worked hard all year, and you need a break. You probably want to book a ticket and head to the beach. But before you book it, stop and think. Maybe this year, you could do something different. You could **volunteer** for one of hundreds of programs around the world, and have a vacation to remember.

1. Helping wildlife in the Galapagos Islands

The Galapagos Islands are on the equator, 1,000 kilometers west of Ecuador, in South America. They're famous for their **biodiversity**. Unfortunately, plants and animals in the Galapagos Islands are in danger, partly because of tourism. However, you could volunteer for a project to help. You will plant trees and look after giant tortoises.

giant tortoise

reef shark

2. Helping shark conservation in Fiji

Fiji is a group of islands about 2,000 kilometers northeast of New Zealand, and scientists are working on ways to protect reef sharks there. Sharks are scary, right? Sure, but they're also in danger. Because of pollution and global warming, sharks are now eating a lot of plastic waste and having to swim in water that is warmer than normal. You could help them by learning how to identify and **tag** sharks—to put an electronic tag on them. Don't worry, it's safe! You will also learn how to **dive**—which can be really fun!

3. Building a library in Ghana

Ghana is in West Africa and has a population of 30 million. It's a **fascinating** country with friendly people. They need volunteers to help build more schools and libraries. Don't worry—you don't need to know about **construction** work. There are a lot of simple jobs you could do. And you will get the chance to stay with a family and eat delicious Ghanaian food.

2 **Read the article and answer the questions.**

1. Which group of islands is farther away from the nearest country?
2. Why is there a problem in the Galapagos?
3. Why are sharks in Fiji in danger?
4. Why do they need volunteers in Ghana?

3 **Find these phrases in the article and answer the questions.**

1. *... before you book **it** ...* (lines 3–4)	Before you book what?
2. ***They're** famous for their biodiversity.* (lines 9–10)	What are famous?
3. *... you could volunteer for a project to help.* (lines 11–12)	To help what?
4. *... you could help **them** ...* (line 19)	Help who?
5. *Don't worry, **it's** safe!* (lines 20–21)	What's safe?
6. ***They** need volunteers to help build ...* (lines 24–25)	Who needs volunteers?

4 GROUP WORK **Discuss the three projects. Which one do you like best? Why?**

WRITING Turn to page 113.

SPEAKING *What next?*

1 PAIR WORK **Play the game. Ask and answer questions.**

- Student A rolls a dice and moves to that number square.
- Student B asks a question, and then a follow-up question.
- Switch roles. Repeat at least three times. Go back up to square 1 if you have to move beyond the last sqare.

Number 2. Do you think you'll work in an office next year?

No, I don't.

Why not?

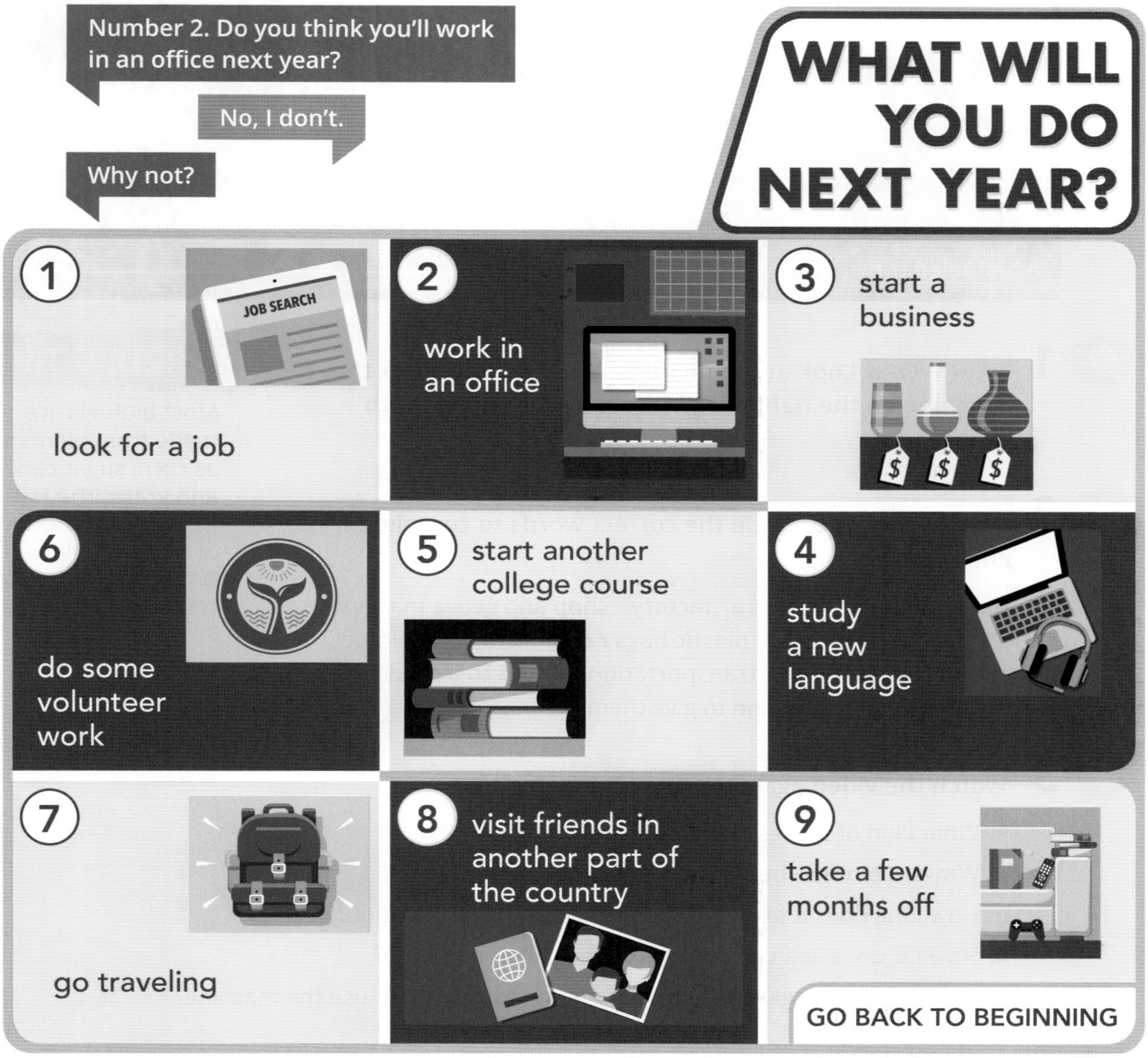

2 GROUP WORK **Tell another pair about your partner's answers. Ask and answer questions for more information.**

3 OVER TO YOU **Find out more about interesting volunteer programs in your country.**

GO ONLINE for grammar, vocabulary, and speaking practice

NOW I CAN

SPEAKING	GRAMMAR	LISTENING	READING
☐ talk about future plans	☐ use modals for possibility, speculation, and deduction.	☐ listen to people talking about careers and studying abroad.	☐ understand a text about volunteering on vacation.

VIDEO

1 PAIR WORK Look at the pictures. What do you think the machine on the right does? Discuss your answer with your partner.

2 Watch the video. Circle the correct words to complete the summary.

In the video, Sean visits a [1] **factory / shop** and gets a machine that can convert used [2] **plastic bags / cooking oil** into biofuel. He then [3] **takes public transportation / drives** to a children's home in [4] **Cambodia / Thailand** to give them the machine.

3 Watch the video again. Answer the questions.

1. What kind of stories does Sean cover in his work?
2. Why are biofuels better than fossil fuels?
3. How long does it take to convert the cooking oil into biofuel?
4. How far does Sean drive to get to the children's home?
5. What does Sean give the children's home to help them use the machine?

4 PAIR WORK Number the transportation 1–5, from most to least eco-friendly. Discuss your answers with a partner. Give reasons.

☐ bus ☐ car ☐ electric bike ☐ kayak ☐ plane

I think the kayak must be number 1.

So do I. If you travel by kayak, you don't cause any pollution.

CULTURE TIP

Most biofuels are made from plants such as corn, sugar cane, and grass. The USA is the largest producer of biofuel, followed by Brazil. Together, these countries produce over 70% of the world's biofuel.

READING

1 PAIR WORK Look at the title of the article. What advice do you expect to read?

TIPS FOR BEING A GREEN TRAVELER

If you follow this simple travel advice, you could help make a big difference to the environment.

1 Think about ____________________

Over 1.4 billion people travel internationally each year. But do you really need to travel abroad to have a great vacation? There must be lots of amazing places in your own country that you haven't visited. If you travel fewer kilometers, your trip will be greener. You might also be surprised at what you discover.

2 Think about ____________________

If it's possible, of course it's better to use public transportation to get to your vacation destination. When you arrive, try to get around by bike or on foot. You're on vacation, so you can't be in a hurry. Take time to enjoy what's around you!

3 Think about ____________________

Avoid traveling on busy days, such as public holidays or the first day of summer vacation. If you travel by road on these days, your trip will take longer and your vehicle will use more fuel. You'll save time and money if you leave a few days earlier or later. You might also be less stressed when you arrive.

4 Think about ____________________

If you pack less, your luggage will be lighter. And if your luggage is lighter, your transportation will be less heavy and more efficient. But don't forget to pack a reusable water bottle and shopping bag. You'll produce much less plastic waste if you don't need to buy bottled water or single-use bags.

5 Think about ____________________

Try to find a hotel which uses renewable energy, recycles, and uses eco-friendly cleaning products. And you could help, too. Your towels and sheets don't need changing every day. If you reuse them, the hotel will be able to save water and energy.

2 Read the article. Complete the headings with phrases from the box below. Which two didn't you use?

why you travel	where you stay	who you take	where you go
when you travel	how you travel	what you take	

3 GROUP WORK Which of the advice in the article do you follow when you go on vacation?

> I didn't use to care about buying plastic bottles of water, but now I have a reusable bottle. I take it everywhere I go.

SMART TALK **UNIT 1** *How are you different?*

Student A

1 Complete the chart with information about you. Then add your own question.

QUESTIONS	YOU	YOUR PARTNER
1 What places do you like going to on vacation? (beach/mountains/cities etc.)		
3 Do you like traveling alone or in a group?		
5 Where did you go on your first vacation?		
7 (Your choice) ____________ ____________ ____________		

2 PAIR WORK **Ask your partner the questions. Agree or disagree with your partner's answers. Then answer your partner's questions.**

A What places do you like going to on vacation?

B I like beach vacations.

A So do I! / Really? I don't. I like going to cities.

3 GROUP WORK **Complete these sentences to compare you and your partner. Then tell your group.**

1. My partner likes ____________________, and so do I / but I don't.
2. My partner doesn't like ____________________, and neither do I / but I do.
3. My partner's favorite place for a vacation is ____________________, and mine is ____________________.

UNIT 2 *What's interesting and what's boring?*

Student A

1

PAIR WORK Ask your partner questions to complete the chart. Add two activities to the list.

A Do you like watching movies in a movie theater?

B No, it's boring. I prefer watching them on my computer.

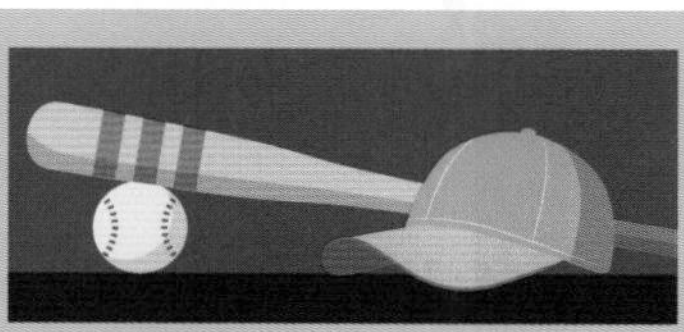

	1 very boring	2 boring	3 OK	4 interesting / exciting	5 very interesting / exciting
1 Watching movies in a theater					
2 Going to live concerts					
3 Going to live sports events					
4 Chatting to people online					
5 Hanging out at shopping malls					
6 Having parties with family					
7 (Your choice) ___________					
8 (Your choice) ___________					

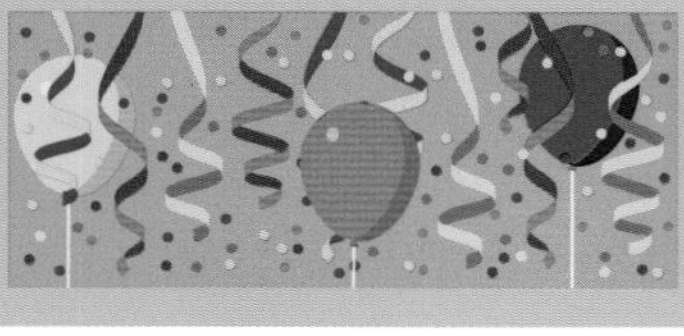

2

PAIR WORK Ask and answer questions about what you and your partner like doing at the following times. Then tell the rest of the class about your partner's likes and dislikes.

What do you like doing ...

- after class?
- on the weekend?
- in the summer?
- on vacation?
- when it's raining?
- alone?
- with your friends?
- with your family?

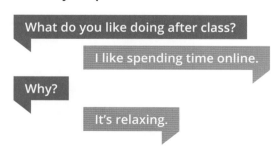

What do you like doing after class?

I like spending time online.

Why?

It's relaxing.

UNIT 3 *Have you ever ... ?*

Student A

1 Answer the questions about you. Try to give extra information!

1. **Have you ever played volleyball?**
   You: ____________________
   Your partner: ____________________

3. **Have you ever spent the night in the hospital?**
   You: ____________________
   Your partner: ____________________

5. **Have you ever taken a long-haul flight?**
   You: ____________________
   Your partner: ____________________

7. **Have you ever climbed a really high mountain?**
   You: ____________________
   Your partner: ____________________

9. **Have you ever eaten Chinese food?**
   You: ____________________
   Your partner: ____________________

2 PAIR WORK Ask and answer questions to complete the information about your partner. Ask for details.

Have you ever played volleyball?

Yes, I have. I played on vacation last year.

Really? Where did you play?

On a beach. It was fun!

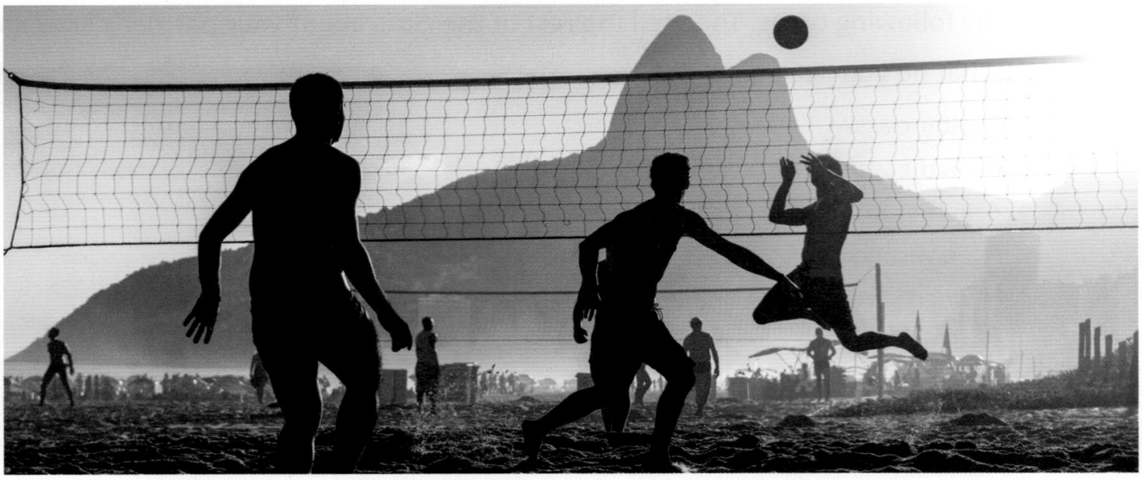

UNIT 4 *The superlative quiz*

Student A

1 Complete the chart with your information and opinion about each topic. Then ask your partner.

What was your best subject at school?

Math. What was yours?

Topics	You	Your partner
1 My best school subject	______	______
3 Most boring place in our city	______	______
5 Most talented friend	______	______
7 Best places to eat in our town	______	______
9 Most boring TV show	______	______
11 Most difficult thing about English	______	______
13 Best sports team in this country	______	______
15 Most interesting day of my life	______	______

2 GROUP WORK Share and compare your answers with another pair.

UNIT 5 *Dragon boats*

Student A

1 PAIR WORK **Read the facts about the Hong Kong dragon boat races. Take turns asking questions and answering your partner's questions.**

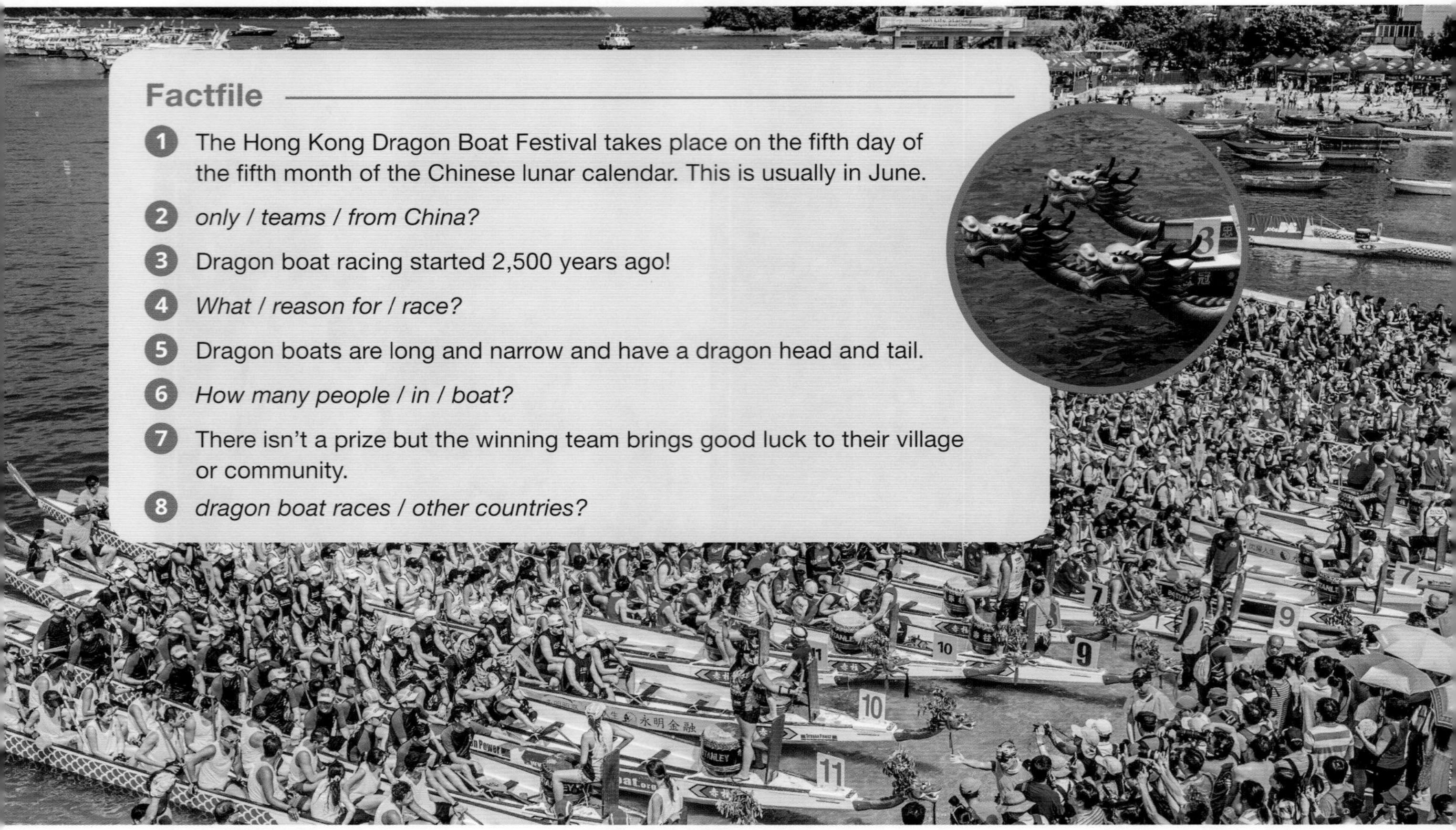

Factfile

1. The Hong Kong Dragon Boat Festival takes place on the fifth day of the fifth month of the Chinese lunar calendar. This is usually in June.
2. *only / teams / from China?*
3. Dragon boat racing started 2,500 years ago!
4. *What / reason for / race?*
5. Dragon boats are long and narrow and have a dragon head and tail.
6. *How many people / in / boat?*
7. There isn't a prize but the winning team brings good luck to their village or community.
8. *dragon boat races / other countries?*

2 PAIR WORK **Discuss the idea of dragon boat races. Describe the races and the people in the boats.**

UNIT 6 *Help! Is this true?*

Student A

1 Read the advice. Do you know if it's right or wrong? Check (✓) one of the boxes for each piece of advice.

1. You should stretch before you exercise.
   ☐ Right ☐ Wrong ☐ I don't know
2. You shouldn't eat before you exercise.
   ☐ Right ☐ Wrong ☐ I don't know
3. You should wait for twelve hours between your evening meal and breakfast the next day.
   ☐ Right ☐ Wrong ☐ I don't know
4. You should drink regularly during the day.
   ☐ Right ☐ Wrong ☐ I don't know
5. You should work out in the morning.
   ☐ Right ☐ Wrong ☐ I don't know
6. You should exercise seven days a week.
   ☐ Right ☐ Wrong ☐ I don't know

2 PAIR WORK **Now read the information about 1, 3, and 5. Then answer your partner's questions and ask for information about 2, 4, and 6.**

1. Should you stretch before you exercise?
   No. Stretching is not good before running or weight lifting. It's better to swing your arms and legs.
2. Should you or shouldn't you eat before you exercise? ______________________
3. Should you wait for twelve hours between your evening meal and breakfast the next day?
   Definitely! This way, you eat during a twelve-hour period and you "fast" (don't eat) during a twelve-hour period.
4. Should you drink regularly during the day? ______________________
5. Should you work out in the morning?
   For some people, morning exercise is good. But it isn't better than exercise in the afternoon or evening. People should exercise when they want to. But don't exercise just before bedtime!
6. Should you exercise seven days a week? ______________________

3 PAIR WORK **Discuss these questions.**

1. Did you learn anything new from this activity? What?
2. Are you surprised by any of the answers? Which?
3. Are you going to change your habits? How?

UNIT 7 *Shopper's paradise?*

Student A

1 PAIR WORK **Read about Khan El Khalili Bazaar. Then answer your partner's questions.**

KHAN EL KHALILI BAZAAR

Khan El Khalili is a *souk* in Cairo, Egypt. *Souk* is the Arabic word for market.

The market opened in 1382 when a prince named El-Khalili built it. At the beginning, they sold silk and spices from the Far East. Now you can buy anything. It's a good place to buy clothes, which are usually very cheap.

There are also some of Cairo's most interesting and oldest cafes, including the El-Fishawi, which opened in 1797.

Tourists love Khan El Khalili, but some local people think that it is now too crowded.

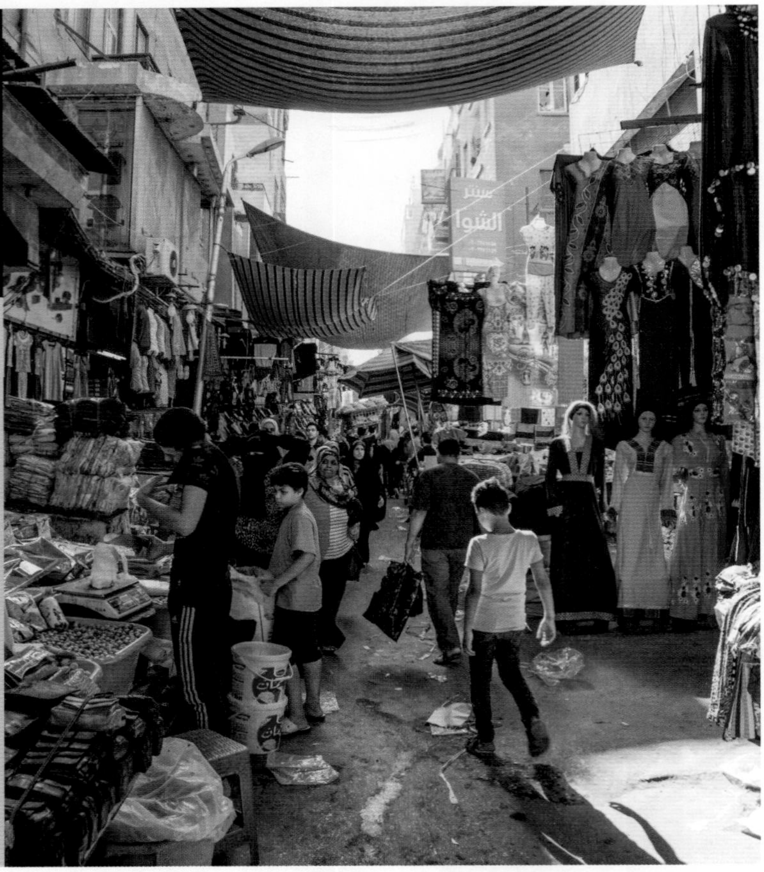

2 PAIR WORK **Ask your partner about Chatuchak Weekend Market.**

1. Chatuchak Weekend Market is the most famous market in ____________ . (*Where is it?*)
2. There are more than ____________ stalls. (*How many ... ?*)
3. Every day more than ____________ people visit the market.
4. They spend about ____________ there each day.
5. The best time to visit is ____________ .
6. The vendors only accept ____________ as payment.

3 PAIR WORK **Do you know another interesting place to shop? Tell your partner.**

UNIT 8 *Making connections*

Student A

1 PAIR WORK **Ask and answer questions to complete the information.**

A What languages does Danielle study?
B Japanese and Mandarin Chinese.

A What's she interested in?
B Robots.

Making connections

The website where you can connect with people who have similar interests

1 Danielle

From the US
Speaks English and Spanish
Studies Japanese and Mandarin Chinese
Interested in robots

2 Hans

From Canada
Speaks English and French
Studies Spanish and Portuguese
Interested in motorcycles

3 Isabel

From Mexico
Speaks Spanish and English
Studies ____________
Interested in ____________

4 Adam

From Great Britain
Speaks English and German
Studies ____________
Interested in ____________

5 Andrea

From Brazil
Speaks Portuguese and English
Studies German and French
Interested in extreme sports

6 Bruce

From Australia
Speaks English and Indonesian
Studies Mandarin Chinese and German
Interested in history

7 Yukiko

From Japan
Speaks Japanese and English
Studies ____________
Interested in ____________

8 Antonio

From Peru
Speaks Spanish and English
Studies Japanese and Korean
Interested in robots

2 PAIR WORK **Who can each person connect with?**

Danielle can practice Japanese with ____________ and Chinese with ____________, and she can talk about robots with ____________.

UNIT 9 *What happened?*

Student A

1 PAIR WORK **Ask and answer questions to complete the information.**

B What's Aya's problem?

A She broke her hand.

B How did she do it?

A She was riding her bicycle and she fell off.

1 Aya

Problem: broke her hand

What happened? She was riding her bicycle and she fell off.

2 Sam

Problem: ______________

What happened? ______________

3 Mariella

Problem: ______________

What happened? ______________

4 Suki

Problem: dislocated a finger

What happened? She was playing tennis. She hit her finger with her racket.

5 James

Problem: got a black eye

What happened? He was boxing with a friend at the gym. His friend hit his eye.

6 Tommy

Problem: ______________

What happened? ______________

7 Roberto

Problem ______________

What happened? ______________

8 Ana Pilar

Problem: cut her finger

What happened? She was cutting some vegetables in the kitchen. She cut her finger.

UNIT 10 *Before they were famous*

Student A

1 Mark the sentences *T* (true) or *F* (false). Guess the answers you don't know.

TRUE OR FALSE?

1 Tennis players Venus and Serena Williams used to write a tennis newsletter when they were younger. ____

2 Actor Daniel Radcliffe used to write poetry while he was filming the *Harry Potter* movies, and he has published a book of poems. ____

3 Movie director Quentin Tarantino used to work in a video store. ____

4 Singer Madonna used to work in a donut shop in New York City. ____

5 Actor Ashton Kutcher used to work in a cereal factory. ____

6 Tennis player Roger Federer used to play professional soccer. ____

7 Actor Leonardo DiCaprio used to appear in TV advertisements for bubble gum. ____

8 Fashion designer Victoria Beckham used to sing with a band called The Spice Girls. ____

Venus and Serena Williams

2 PAIR WORK **Tell your partner your answers. Then use the information below to check your partner's answers.**

1. True: Actor John Cho used to teach English at a high school.
2. True: Actor Charlize Theron used to take care of the animals on her parents' farm.
3. True: Soccer player Neymar used to play for the Brazilian club Santos, the same team that Pelé played for.
4. False: Singer Rihanna didn't use to speak French at home when she was a child.
5. True: Ariana Grande used to eat meat, but now she's vegan.
6. True: Japanese Empress Masako used to be a star athlete at school.
7. True: Tennis player Rafael Nadal's uncle used to play soccer for Barcelona.
8. True: Film star Emma Stone used to work in a bakery that made dog food.

3 PAIR WORK **Do you know what other celebrities used to do before they were famous? Tell your partner.**

UNIT 11 *Making houses from plastic bottles*

Student A

1 Read Text A to answer the questions from Student B.

A

More than 15 years ago, German ecologist and engineer Andreas Froese had an idea: Why not build homes with plastic bottles? His company has now built more than 50 houses around the world. A typical house needs 14,000 plastic bottles. It costs a quarter of the cost of a normal home. The Ecotec house in El Zamorano, in Honduras, is the most famous of his houses. It's very easy to build a plastic bottle house. The builders fill the bottles with sand; then they make a wall with them and put mud or cement between them. Plastic bottle walls are much stronger than brick walls.

The Ecotec house in El Zamorano, in Honduras.

2 Now ask Student B questions 1–6 to complete text B.

B

[1]___________ (*which country?*) is another country where people are building homes with plastic bottles. In that country, they throw away [2]___________ (*how many?*) plastic bottles every year. They are building [3]___________ (*how many?*) plastic bottle houses in the village of Yelwa. They need about [4]___________ (*how many?*) bottles to build a home, and the bottles must be the same size. Finding the right bottles is the most difficult part of the process! [5]___________ (*who?*) give bottles to the builders. The builders then fill the bottles with [6]___________ (*what?*).

The first bottle home in the village of Yelwa, in ___________ (*which country?*)

3 GROUP WORK Talk about any buildings you know that use recycled materials. Would you live in a building made with recycled materials? Why or why not?

UNIT 12 *What are your plans?*

Student A

1 PAIR WORK **Ask questions to find out about Tony's plans after college. Then answer questions about Lisa's plans.**

A: What is Tony going to do? **B:** He's going to ____________

So, Tony, it's the end of the semester. What are you going to do when you leave college?
I'm not sure, Lisa.
I'm going to [1]____________ . If I don't get one, I might [2]____________ .
I may buy one of those all-access train tickets and travel all around [3]____________ .
That sounds fun.
What about you? What are your plans?
I applied for a job with an environmental charity.
Wow! Excellent!
If I get the job, I'll go to South America.
You must be excited. What will you do there?
I'll help the charity build a hospital.
Maybe I could do something like that.
Yes, why not?

2 PAIR WORK **What are your study and / or work plans for next year? Tell your partner.**

SMART TALK UNIT 1 *How are you different?*

Student B

1 **Complete the chart with information about you. Then add your own question.**

QUESTIONS	YOU	YOUR PARTNER
2 What do you like doing best on vacation? (going to the beach, visiting famous places, etc.)		
4 What don't you like doing on vacation?		
6 What's your favorite way to travel? (plane, train, car, etc.)		
8 (Your choice) ________ ________ ________		

2 PAIR WORK **Ask your partner the questions. Agree or disagree with your partner's answers. Then answer your partner's questions.**

B What do you like doing best on vacation?

A I like going to the beach.

B So do I! / Really? I don't. I like visiting famous places.

3 GROUP WORK **Complete these sentences to compare you and your partner. Then tell your group.**

1. My partner likes ________________, and so do I / but I don't.
2. My partner doesn't like ________________, and neither do I / but I do.
3. My partner's favorite place for a vacation is ________________, and mine is ________________.

UNIT 2 *What's interesting and what's boring?*

Student B

1

PAIR WORK Ask your partner questions to complete the chart. Add two activities to the list.

B Do you like watching movies on your computer?

A No, it's boring. I prefer going to movie theaters.

	1 very boring	2 boring	3 OK	4 interesting / exciting	5 very interesting / exciting
1 Watching movies on your computer					
2 Watching music videos					
3 Watching live sports on TV					
4 Texting your friends					
5 Hanging out in cafes					
6 Visiting family members					
7 (Your choice) ______					
8 (Your choice) ______					

2

PAIR WORK Ask and answer questions about what you and your partner like doing at the following times. Then tell the rest of the class about your partner's likes and dislikes.

What do you like doing ...

- after class?
- on the weekend?
- in the summer?
- on vacation?
- when it's raining?
- alone?
- with your friends?
- with your family?

What do you like doing after class?

I like watching music videos.

Why?

It's relaxing.

UNIT 3 *Have you ever … ?*

Student B

1 First answer the questions about you. Add extra information.

2 **Have you ever been bungee-jumping?**

You: ______________________

Your partner: ______________________

4 **Have you ever been to an all-night party?**

You: ______________________

Your partner: ______________________

6 **Have you ever gotten sick in a car, bus, boat, or plane?**

You: ______________________

Your partner: ______________________

8 **Have you ever played baseball?**

You: ______________________

Your partner: ______________________

10 **Have you ever eaten something really strange?**

You: ______________________

Your partner: ______________________

2 PAIR WORK Now ask and answer questions to complete the information about your partner. Ask for details.

Have you ever been bungee-jumping?

Yes, I have.

Really? Where did you do it?

On vacation in New Zealand.

UNIT 4 *The superlative quiz*

Student B

1 Complete the chart with your information and opinion about each topic. Then ask your partner.

What was your worst subject at school?
History. What was yours?

	Topics	You	Your partner
2	My worst school subject	__________	__________
4	Most interesting place in our city	__________	__________
6	Funniest friend	__________	__________
8	Worst places to eat in our town	__________	__________
10	Most interesting TV show	__________	__________
12	Easiest thing about English	__________	__________
14	Worst sports team in this country	__________	__________
16	Most boring day of my life	__________	__________

2 GROUP WORK Share and compare your answers with another pair.

UNIT 5 *Dragon boats*

Student B

1 PAIR WORK **Read the facts about the Hong Kong dragon boat races. Take turns asking questions and answering your partner's questions.**

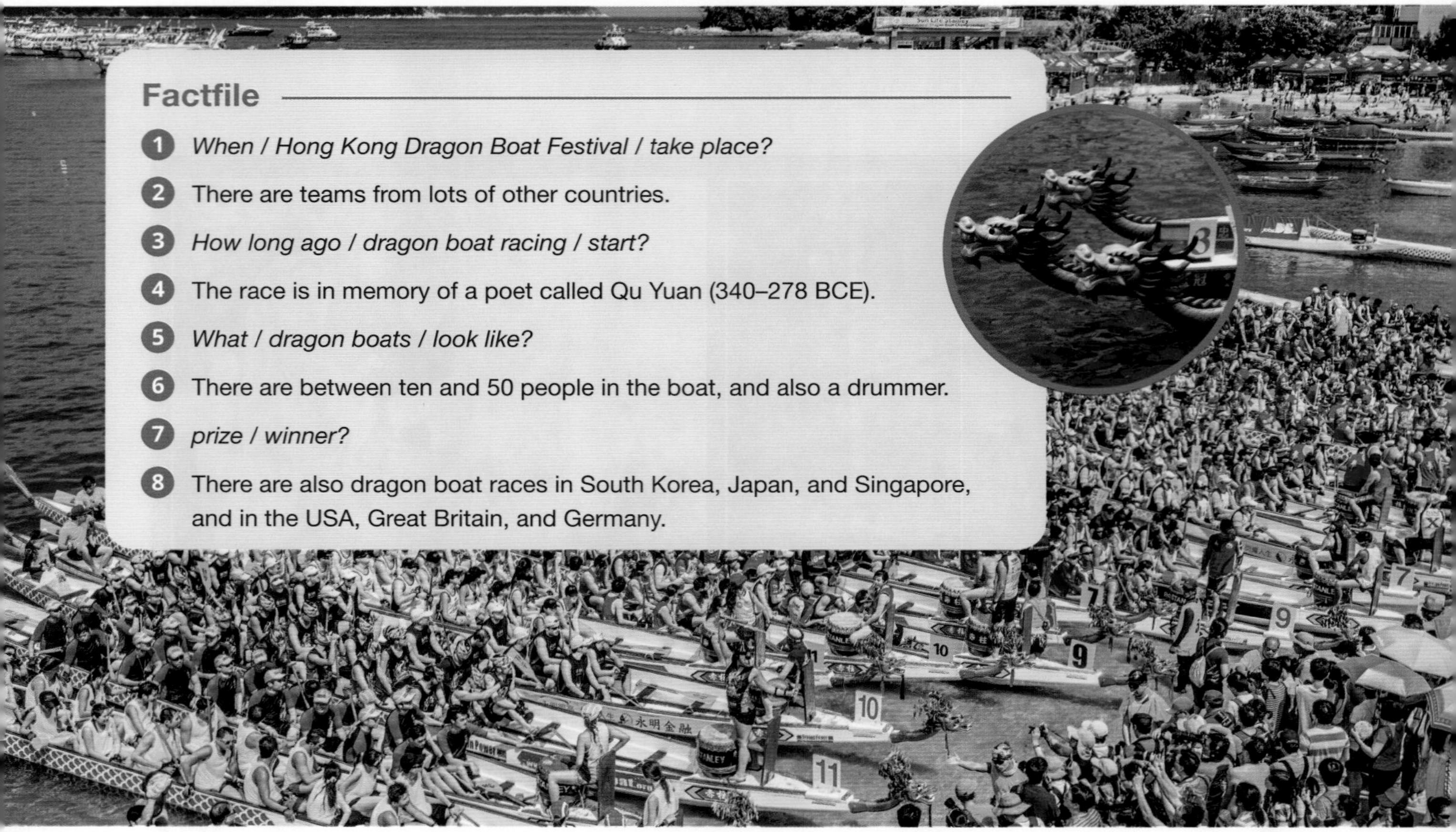

Factfile

1. *When / Hong Kong Dragon Boat Festival / take place?*
2. There are teams from lots of other countries.
3. *How long ago / dragon boat racing / start?*
4. The race is in memory of a poet called Qu Yuan (340–278 BCE).
5. *What / dragon boats / look like?*
6. There are between ten and 50 people in the boat, and also a drummer.
7. *prize / winner?*
8. There are also dragon boat races in South Korea, Japan, and Singapore, and in the USA, Great Britain, and Germany.

2 PAIR WORK **Discuss the idea of dragon boat races. Describe the races and the people in the boats.**

UNIT 6 *Help! Is this true?*

Student B

1 Read the advice. Do you know if it's right or wrong? Check (✓) one of the boxes for each piece of advice.

1. You should stretch before you exercise.
   ▢ Right ▢ Wrong ▢ I don't know
2. You shouldn't eat before you exercise.
   ▢ Right ▢ Wrong ▢ I don't know
3. You should wait for twelve hours between your evening meal and breakfast the next day.
   ▢ Right ▢ Wrong ▢ I don't know
4. You should drink regularly during the day.
   ▢ Right ▢ Wrong ▢ I don't know
5. You should work out in the morning.
   ▢ Right ▢ Wrong ▢ I don't know
6. You should exercise seven days a week.
   ▢ Right ▢ Wrong ▢ I don't know

2 PAIR WORK **Now read the information about 2, 4, and 6. Then answer your partner's questions and ask for information about 1, 3, and 5.**

1. Should you stretch before you exercise? ____________________
2. Should you or shouldn't you eat before you exercise?
   You should eat normally before you exercise, but don't exercise immediately after eating. People think that if they don't eat, they burn more fat when they exercise. This isn't true. Exercising on an empty stomach is like driving a car without gasoline.
3. Should you wait for twelve hours between your evening meal and breakfast the next day?
   ____
4. Should you drink regularly during the day?
   You should drink regularly during the day. Your body needs water to work properly.
5. Should you work out in the morning? ____________________
6. Should you exercise seven days a week?
   Regular exercise is very good, but exercising seven days a week isn't necessary. In fact, it's better to take a day or two off every week.

3 PAIR WORK **Discuss these questions.**

1. Did you learn anything new from this activity? What?
2. Are you surprised by any of the answers? Which?
3. Are you going to change your habits? How?

UNIT 7 *Shopper's paradise?*

Student B

1 PAIR WORK Read about Chatuchak Weekend Market. Then answer your partner's questions.

CHATUCHAK WEEKEND MARKET

Chatuchak Weekend Market is the most famous market in Bangkok, Thailand. There are more than 8,000 stalls, and every day more than 200,000 people visit the market. They spend about $750,000 there each day.

It seems too big, but don't worry! There's a path around the market, and then a system of smaller paths: Soi 1, Soi 2, etc. There's also a very good map to help you.

The best time to visit is early morning or evening because it gets very hot in the middle of the day.

And one more thing – take cash. The vendors don't accept credit cards.

2 Ask your partner about Khan El Khalili Bazaar.

1. Khan El Khalili is a *souk* in ____________ .
   (*Where is it?*)
2. *Souk* is the Arabic word for ____________ .
   (*What does* souk *mean?*)
3. Khan El Khalili opened in ____________ , when a prince built it.
4. At the beginning, they sold ____________ from the Far East.
5. It's a good place to buy clothes because they are usually ____________ .
6. You can drink coffee in Cairo's oldest ____________ in the market.

3 PAIR WORK Do you know another interesting place to shop? Tell your partner.

UNIT 8 *Making connections*

Student B

1 PAIR WORK **Ask and answer questions to complete the information.**

B What languages does Hans study?
A Spanish and Portuguese.

B What's he interested in?
A Motorcycles.

Making connections

The website where you can connect with people who have similar interests

1 Danielle

From the US
Speaks English and Spanish
Studies Japanese and Mandarin Chinese
Interested in robots

2 Hans

From Canada
Speaks English and French
Studies Spanish and Portuguese
Interested in motorcycles

3 Isabel

From Mexico
Speaks Spanish and English
Studies Mandarin Chinese and Portuguese
Interested in extreme sports

4 Adam

From Great Britain
Speaks English and German
Studies Korean and Japanese
Interested in history

5 Andrea

From Brazil
Speaks Portuguese and English
Studies ______________
Interested in ______________

6 Bruce

From Australia
Speaks English and Indonesian
Studies ______________
Interested in ______________

7 Yukiko

From Japan
Speaks Japanese and English
Studies Korean and Mandarin Chinese
Interested in cars and motorcycles

8 Antonio

From Peru
Speaks Spanish and English
Studies ______________
Interested in ______________

2 PAIR WORK **Who can each person connect with?**

Danielle can practice Japanese with ____________ and Chinese with ____________, and she can talk about robots with ____________.

UNIT 9 *What happened?*

Student B

1 **PAIR WORK** **Ask and answer questions to complete the information.**

A What's Sam's problem?

B He lost a tooth

A How did he do it?

B He was playing baseball.

1 Aya

Problem: ____________

What happened? ____________

2 Sam

Problem: lost a tooth

What happened? He was playing baseball and the ball hit him in the mouth.

3 Mariella

Problem: sprained an ankle

What happened? She was climbing a mountain. She tripped over a rock.

4 Suki

Problem: ____________

What happened? ____________

5 James

Problem: ____________

What happened? ____________

6 Tommy

Problem: broke his nose

What happened? He was walking out of a room and the door closed.

7 Roberto

Problem: bruised his leg

What happened? He fell down when he was climbing a tree.

8 Ana Pilar

Problem: ____________

What happened? ____________

UNIT 10 *Before they were famous*

Student B

1 Mark the sentences *T* (true) or *F* (false). Guess the answers you don't know.

TRUE OR FALSE?

1 Actor John Cho used to teach English at a high school. ____

2 Actor Charlize Theron used to take care of the animals on her parents' farm. ____

3 Soccer player Neymar used to play for the Brazilian club Santos, the same team that Pelé played for. ____

4 Singer Rihanna used to speak French at home when she was a child. ____

5 Ariana Grande used to eat meat, but now she's vegan. ____

6 Japanese Empress Masako used to be a star athlete at school. ____

7 Tennis player Rafael Nadal's uncle used to play soccer for Barcelona. ____

8 Film star Emma Stone used to work in a bakery that made dog food. ____

John Cho

2 PAIR WORK **Tell your partner your answers. Then use the information below to check your partner's answers.**

1. True: Tennis players Venus and Serena Williams used to write a tennis newsletter when they were younger.
2. True: Actor Daniel Radcliffe used to write poetry while he was filming the *Harry Potter* movies, and he has published a book of poems.
3. True: Movie director Quentin Tarantino used to work in a video store.
4. True: Singer Madonna used to work in a donut shop in New York City.
5. True: Actor Ashton Kutcher used to sweep cereal dust in a factory.
6. False: Tennis player Roger Federer didn't use to play professional soccer.
7. True: Actor Leonardo DiCaprio used to appear in TV ads for bubble gum.
8. True: Fashion designer Victoria Beckham used to sing with a band called The Spice Girls.

3 PAIR WORK **Do you know what other celebrities used to do before they were famous? Tell your partner.**

UNIT 11 *Making houses from plastic bottles*

Student B

1 Ask Student A questions 1–6 to complete text A.

A

More than 15 years ago, [1]___________ (*nationality?*) ecologist and engineer Andreas Froese had an idea: Why not build homes with plastic bottles? His company has now built more than [2]___________ (*how many?*) houses around the world. A typical house needs [3]___________ (*how many?*) plastic bottles. It costs [4]___________ (*how much?*) of the cost of a normal home. The Ecotec house in El Zamorano, in [5]___________ (*which country?*), is the most famous of his houses. It's very easy to build a plastic bottle house. The builders fill the bottles with [6]___________ (*what?*); then they make a wall with them and put mud or cement between them. Plastic bottle walls are much stronger than brick walls.

The Ecotec house in El Zamorano, in ___________ (*which country?*)

2 Now read Text B to answer the questions from Student A.

B

Nigeria is another country where people are building homes with plastic bottles. In that country, they throw away five hundred million plastic bottles every year. They are building 25 plastic bottle houses in the village of Yelwa. They need about 14,000 bottles to build a home, and the bottles must be the same size. Finding the right bottles is the most difficult part of the process! Hotels and restaurants give bottles to the builders. The builders then fill the bottles with sand.

The first bottle home in the village of Yelwa, in Nigeria.

3 GROUP WORK **Talk about any buildings you know that use recycled materials. Would you live in a building made with recycled materials? Why or why not?**

UNIT 12 *What are your plans?*

Student B

1 PAIR WORK **Answer questions about Tony's plans after college. Then ask questions to find out about Lisa's plans.**

B What are Lisa's plans?

A She applied for a job with ____________

So, Tony, it's the end of the semester. What are you going to do when you leave college?
I'm not sure, Lisa.
I'm going to look for a job. If I don't get one, I might travel.
I may buy one of those all-access train tickets and travel all around Europe.
That sounds fun.
What about you? What are your plans?
I applied for a job with [4] ____________
Wow! Excellent!
If I get the job, I'll [5] ____________
[6] ____________
You must be excited. What will you do there?
Maybe I could do something like that.
Yes, why not?

2 PAIR WORK **What are your study and / or work plans for next year? Tell your partner.**

WRITING

UNIT 1

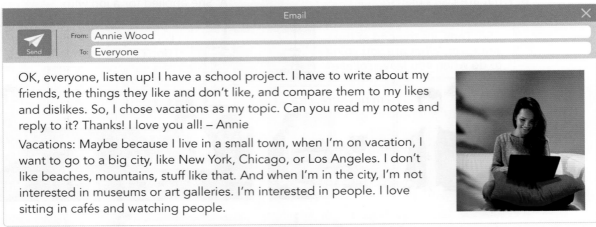

1 **Read the email from Annie to her friends. One of her friends has replied. Imagine you're another friend and write another reply.**

Email

Send | From: Annie Wood
To: Everyone

OK, everyone, listen up! I have a school project. I have to write about my friends, the things they like and don't like, and compare them to my likes and dislikes. So, I chose vacations as my topic. Can you read my notes and reply to it? Thanks! I love you all! – Annie

Vacations: Maybe because I live in a small town, when I'm on vacation, I want to go to a big city, like New York, Chicago, or Los Angeles. I don't like beaches, mountains, stuff like that. And when I'm in the city, I'm not interested in museums or art galleries. I'm interested in people. I love sitting in cafés and watching people.

Email

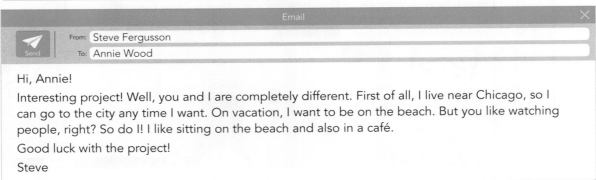

Send | From: Steve Fergusson
To: Annie Wood

Hi, Annie!

Interesting project! Well, you and I are completely different. First of all, I live near Chicago, so I can go to the city any time I want. On vacation, I want to be on the beach. But you like watching people, right? So do I! I like sitting on the beach and also in a café.

Good luck with the project!

Steve

2 PAIR WORK **Compare what you wrote with a partner. How are you different?**

UNIT 2

1 **Read this blog post from a student in the US. Then write a comment to reply. Introduce yourself and answer the questions in the blog.**

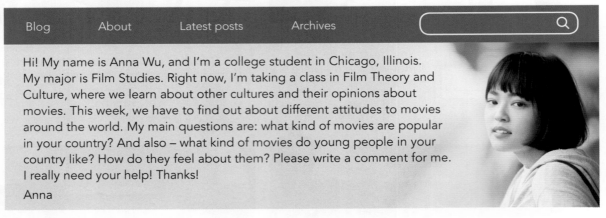

Blog | About | Latest posts | Archives

Hi! My name is Anna Wu, and I'm a college student in Chicago, Illinois. My major is Film Studies. Right now, I'm taking a class in Film Theory and Culture, where we learn about other cultures and their opinions about movies. This week, we have to find out about different attitudes to movies around the world. My main questions are: what kind of movies are popular in your country? And also – what kind of movies do young people in your country like? How do they feel about them? Please write a comment for me. I really need your help! Thanks!

Anna

2 PAIR WORK **Compare your reply with your partner. If your partner has a good idea, add it to your reply.**

UNIT 3

1 **Read these emails between friends who live in different countries. Then write a reply to Jason answering his questions with information about your country.**

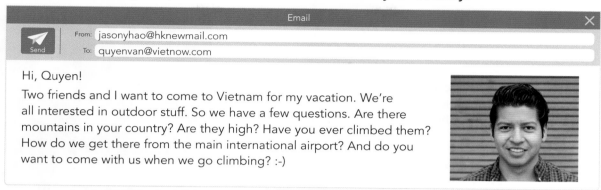

Email

Send From: jasonyhao@hknewmail.com
To: quyenvan@vietnow.com

Hi, Quyen!

Two friends and I want to come to Vietnam for my vacation. We're all interested in outdoor stuff. So we have a few questions. Are there mountains in your country? Are they high? Have you ever climbed them? How do we get there from the main international airport? And do you want to come with us when we go climbing? :-)

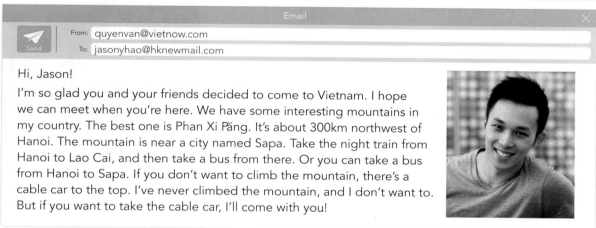

Email

Send From: quyenvan@vietnow.com
To: jasonyhao@hknewmail.com

Hi, Jason!

I'm so glad you and your friends decided to come to Vietnam. I hope we can meet when you're here. We have some interesting mountains in my country. The best one is Phan Xi Păng. It's about 300km northwest of Hanoi. The mountain is near a city named Sapa. Take the night train from Hanoi to Lao Cai, and then take a bus from there. Or you can take a bus from Hanoi to Sapa. If you don't want to climb the mountain, there's a cable car to the top. I've never climbed the mountain, and I don't want to. But if you want to take the cable car, I'll come with you!

2 **PAIR WORK** **Compare your email with a partner. Did you suggest similar things?**

UNIT 4

1 **Read the email from a US student. Then write a description with similar information about your city. Use superlatives if you can!**

Email

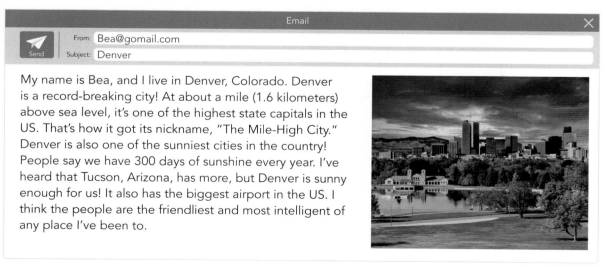

Send From: Bea@gomail.com
Subject: Denver

My name is Bea, and I live in Denver, Colorado. Denver is a record-breaking city! At about a mile (1.6 kilometers) above sea level, it's one of the highest state capitals in the US. That's how it got its nickname, "The Mile-High City." Denver is also one of the sunniest cities in the country! People say we have 300 days of sunshine every year. I've heard that Tucson, Arizona, has more, but Denver is sunny enough for us! It also has the biggest airport in the US. I think the people are the friendliest and most intelligent of any place I've been to.

2 **PAIR WORK** **Compare emails with a partner. Do you agree with your partner's statements?**

UNIT 5

1 Read the description of a birthday party. Then write a description of a party for someone in your family.

Last month was my mom's 40th birthday, and we wanted to give her a surprise party. The problem is — she doesn't like surprises. In the end, I think we did well.

First of all, we booked a table at her favorite restaurant. Just for five people: Mom, Dad, my two sisters, and me. We also booked the table next to our table — a table for six.

When we arrived at the restaurant, the waiter came up to the table and said to my mom: "We know it's your birthday, but don't worry, we aren't going to make a big fuss."

Then, after the waiter went away, the door opened and six people walked into the restaurant. Two of them were my mom's parents, and the other four were her best friends from school. No one said "HAPPY BIRTHDAY!" or stuff like that. She was absolutely delighted.

2 PAIR WORK Compare descriptions of your party with a partner. Are there any similarities or differences?

UNIT 6

1 Read this email. Imagine you have recently started taking a class. Write an email telling a friend what you have learned.

Email

Send

From: Amanda@gomail.com

Subject: Yoga

I took my first yoga class today—and I've already learned a lot!

The first thing I learned is that you should arrive early for class. Everyone in the class got there before I did. By the time I got there, there wasn't much space for me or my mat!

I also found out that you shouldn't eat right before class. I had a big meal an hour before the class, and I was in pain! Believe me, it's hard to do yoga with a very full stomach!

At the end of the class, I got up right away to thank the teacher. I guess you shouldn't do that. She told me that I should close my eyes, breathe deeply, and relax.

I also learned that you don't have to do everything. If something is too difficult, don't do it! Yoga is great. I'm sure I'm going to enjoy it—when my knee stops hurting!

2 PAIR WORK Take turns reading your emails. Ask your partner more about the class.

UNIT 7

1 Read this blog about shopping in San Francisco. Then write about your favorite place to shop.

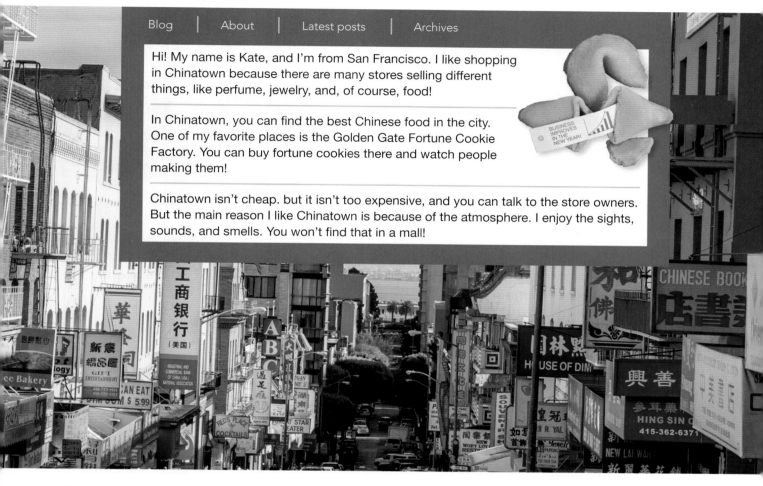

Blog | About | Latest posts | Archives

Hi! My name is Kate, and I'm from San Francisco. I like shopping in Chinatown because there are many stores selling different things, like perfume, jewelry, and, of course, food!

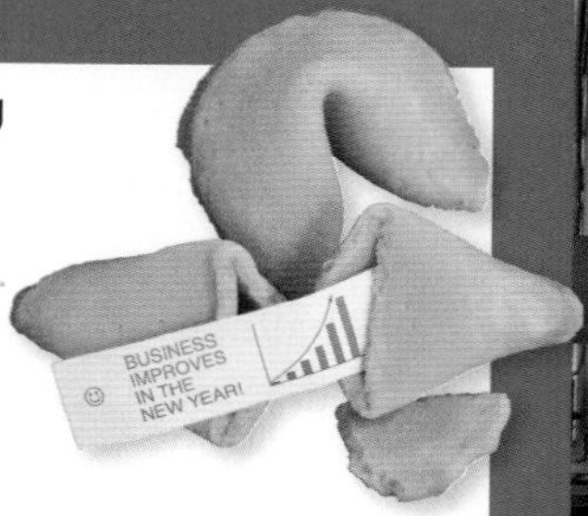

In Chinatown, you can find the best Chinese food in the city. One of my favorite places is the Golden Gate Fortune Cookie Factory. You can buy fortune cookies there and watch people making them!

Chinatown isn't cheap. but it isn't too expensive, and you can talk to the store owners. But the main reason I like Chinatown is because of the atmosphere. I enjoy the sights, sounds, and smells. You won't find that in a mall!

2 PAIR WORK Compare blogs with a partner. Do you have similar shopping preferences?

UNIT 8

1 Read this email from Greengirl33. Then write a similar paragraph about yourself.

Email

Send

From: greengirl33@hmail.com

Subject: My preferences

Hi! I'm a college student who is majoring in Art. I'm living at home with my parents at the moment. I'm very outgoing and people say I'm a talented artist. I like people who are interested in the environment. In terms of entertainment, I prefer movies which have a message, something that makes you think, you know? I like music that makes me feel happy. My favorite kind of food? That's easy—I love Thai food, especially pad Thai!

2 PAIR WORK Compare paragraphs with a partner. What do you have in common?

UNIT 9

1 **Read this paragraph. Then write a similar paragraph about a funny, strange, or interesting thing that happened to you.**

A funny thing happened to me last week. I was coming out of my apartment building when one of my neighbors yelled down to me. "You have to help me," she shouted. "I'm locked in my bathroom!" I didn't really know what to do. I told her to wait while I went for help. I ran until I found a police officer who was giving directions to a tourist. I told him about the woman in the bathroom. He made a phone call, and a few minutes later, a fire engine arrived.

2 PAIR WORK **Compare paragraphs with a partner. Write down two or three questions to ask for more information.**

- Why were you (e.g., waiting for the bus)?
- What happened (e.g., after you spoke to the man)?
- Who was the woman (e.g., who spoke to you)?
- Where did this happen?

UNIT 10

1 **Read these comments on the *Past Times* website. Write a comment about something unusual your parents or grandparents used to do.**

Home | News | Sports | Weather | Video   Search

This week: Strange stuff your folks used to do!

My grandparents' car didn't have seatbelts. When my mom was sitting in the front seat and her dad braked, he used to put his hand out to stop her from hitting the windshield!
Bobby, New York City

When my dad was seven, his parents used to take him and his friends to a movie theater, give them some money, and come back a few hours later to take them home.
Dinah, Orlando, Florida

My mom used to ride her bicycle to school when she was eight years old. The school was five miles away, and she didn't use to wear a helmet!
Grant, Sydney, Australia

2 PAIR WORK **Compare what you wrote with a partner. Who wrote the more unusual comment?**

UNIT 11

1 Read this email from a friend in another country who needs help. Then write a reply. If necessary, use books or go online to find information.

Email

From: leo@smartmail.com

Subject: Important local environmental issues in different countries

Help! I need to finish a project on local environmental issues, and I'm writing to my friends in different countries. Can you answer these questions about the important issues in your area?

1. What are the most important environmental problems in your area? Are there any in this list?
   - air pollution
   - public transportation
   - trees and forests
   - recycling
   - noise
2. Are there any local reasons for the problems? For example:
   - local factories
   - old buses / trains
   - deforestation
   - no recycling centers
   - traffic noise

I would love information about other environmental issues, also. Thanks for your help!

Leo

2 PAIR WORK Take turns reading your emails. Did you agree on what is important in your local area?

UNIT 12

1 Read this message. Imagine you know the writer from social media. Write a reply, answering all the questions.

Hi,

My name is Rolf, and I come from Switzerland. I've seen you on social media, so I hope you don't mind my writing to you like this. I have the chance to come to your country and work on a farm. I'm really interested in animals, and it's a great opportunity, but I need to know a few things before I decide.

Could you answer these questions for me?

I speak French, German, and my English is pretty good, but I don't speak your language. Do you think I can communicate with the people on the farm? I also want to travel to the capital city. Are your trains good? Are they expensive? Are there student hostels in the capital? Are they expensive? Also, I'm a vegetarian. Do you have any vegetarian dishes in your country?

Do you live near the capital? Could we meet when I'm there?

Sorry about all the questions. I hope you can answer them.

Rolf Schweiz

2 PAIR WORK Compare replies with a partner. Did you answer Rolf's questions in the same way?

GRAMMAR

UNIT 1

Agreeing with *so* and *neither*

We use *so* to show agreement with affirmative statements. Notice that we use the verb before the subject.

- *A I'm tired.*
- *B So am I. (~~**So I am.**~~)*
- *A She is hungry.*
- *B So is he. (~~**So he is**~~.)*

We use *neither* to show agreement with negative statements. Notice that we use the verb before the subject.

- *A I'm not thirsty*
- *B Neither am I. (~~**Neither I am**~~.)*
- *A She isn't angry.*
- *B Neither is he. (~~**Neither he is**~~.)*

We use the helping verbs *be, can,* and *do* with *so* and *neither*.

So	Neither
A I'**m** studying now.	**A** I'**m** not studying now.
B So **am** I.	**B** Neither **am** I.
A I'**m** going to leave soon.	**A** I'**m not** going to leave soon.
B So **am** I.	**B** Neither **am** I.
A I **can** swim.	**A** I **can't** swim.
B So **can** I.	**B** Neither **can** I.
A I **like** mountain climbing.	**A** I **don't like** mountain climbing.
B So **do** I.	**B** Neither **do** I.
A I **talked** to him yesterday.	**A** I **didn't talk** to him yesterday.
B So **did** I.	**B** Neither **did** I.

There is also a more informal way to respond.

- *A I'm going on vacation.* *B Me too.*
- *A I'm not going on vacation.* *B Me neither.*

Disagreeing

Notice that when we disagree, we use the helping verb after the subject.

- *A I'm going on vacation.* *B Really? **I'm not**.*
- *A I don't want to go.* *B Well, **I do**.*

NOW PRACTICE

1 **Agree or disagree with the statements below.**

1. **A** We loved the movie.
   B __So did__ we.
2. **A** I don't understand this.
   B __________ I.
3. **A** She can't leave now.
   B Well, he ____________ .
4. **A** I'm going to take a vacation soon.
   B Well, he __________ .
5. **A** I think hiking is boring.
   B Really? We __________ .
6. **A** We didn't go scuba diving.
   B ____________ we.
7. **A** He can come for dinner.
   B __________ she.
8. **A** I'm not going to stay out late tonight.
   B Well, I ____________ .
9. **A** We don't like going to parties.
   B Really? We __________ .
10. **A** She isn't saying anything.
    B ____________ he.

UNIT 2

Adjectives with *-ing* and *-ed*; *-ed* adjectives + preposition

We usually use adjectives ending with *-ed* to describe feelings or emotions.

- *I feel tir**ed**. (~~**I feel tiring**~~.)*
- *I feel relax**ed**. (~~**I feel relaxing**~~.)*
- *I feel bor**ed**. (~~**I feel boring**~~.)*
- *I feel disappoint**ed**. (~~**I feel disappointing**~~.)*

We usually use adjectives ending with *-ing* to describe the causes of feelings or emotions.

- *Hiking is tir**ing**. (~~**Hiking is tired**~~.)*
- *The movie is bor**ing**. (~~**The movie is bored**~~.)*
- *Sailing is relax**ing**. (~~**Sailing is relaxed**~~.)*
- *The music was disappoint**ing**. (~~**The music was disappointed**~~.)*

After some *-ed* adjectives, we can use a preposition + a noun or gerund (the *-ing* form of a verb).

- *I am interested **in your new book**.*
- *I am interested **in reading your new book**.*

Some common *-ed* adjectives + prepositions are:

-ed adjective	+ preposition
amazed	at
annoyed	by / with
bored	with
disappointed	in / with
excited	about / by

-ed adjective	+ preposition
frightened	of / by
interested	in
surprised	by / at
terrified	of / at
tired	of

NOW PRACTICE

1 **Complete the conversations. Choose the correct word in parentheses.**

1. A How was the movie?
   B It was OK, but I was (*boring* / *bored*) for the first hour.
2. A How was your sailing trip?
   B It was (*frightening* / *frightened*). I almost fell in the water.
3. A Do you want to go out tonight?
   B I don't think so. I feel really (*tiring* / *tired*).
4. A How was the party?
   B It was really (*disappointing* / *disappointed*). Only a few people came.
5. A Did you enjoy your vacation?
   B Absolutely. It was (*amazing* / *amazed*).

2 **Complete the questions with a preposition from the box. More than one answer may be possible.**

about	by	in	of

1. Do you ever get tired ____________ watching movies?
2. What are you interested ____________ doing this weekend?
3. Do you ever get excited ____________ doing your homework?
4. What are most people terrified ____________ ?
5. In the library I'm often annoyed ____________ people talking.
6. Why are some people frightened ____________ airplanes?

UNIT 3

The present perfect

We use the present perfect:

1. to talk about a past event which happened in a period of time up to now.
   - ***Have you*** *ever* ***ridden*** *a motorcycle? (= in your life up to now)*
   - *She* ***has climbed*** *ten mountains. (= in her life up to now)*
2. to connect the past with the present.
   - *I* ***have forgotten*** *my homework. (= I don't have it now.)*
   - *He* ***has broken*** *his arm. (= It is broken now.)*
   - *I* ***have studied*** *English for five months. (= I'm still studying English.)*
   - *We* ***have lived*** *in Seoul since 2009. (= We are still living in Seoul.)*

We form the present perfect with *has / have* + the past participle of the main verb.

Affirmative and negative statements					
I You We They	**have** **'ve** **have not** **haven't**	**tried** it.	He She It	**has** **'s** **has not** **hasn't**	**tried** it.

We don't mention the exact time of a past event when we use the present perfect. But we can use time expressions for periods of time up to now that are not finished yet. When we are talking about a specific time in the past, we use the simple past form of a verb.

- *We****'ve been*** *there* ***many times****. (= in our lives up to now)*
- *I* ***have climbed*** *three mountains* ***this year****. (= This year is not finished yet.)*
- *I* ***climbed*** *three mountains* ***last year****. (= Last year is over.)*

Note that the present perfect forms of *go* (*been* and *gone*) have different meanings.

- *John* ***has been*** *to Colombia. (He went to Colombia and came back.)*
- *John* ***has gone*** *to Colombia. (He's in Colombia now.)*

NOW PRACTICE

1 Complete the sentences. Use the present perfect form of the verb in parentheses.

1. My sister ______has been______ to Paris. (go)
2. I ____________________ windsurfing. Have you? (not try)
3. We ____________________ anything today. (not eat)
4. He ________________ a sports car. (drive)
5. How many times __________ you __________ in an airplane? (fly)

2 Complete the sentences. Choose the correct form of the verb in parentheses.

1. I *(have been / went)* bungee jumping many times.
2. My friends and I *(have gone / went)* hang-gliding last fall.
3. My parents *(have visited / visited)* China several times last year.
4. We *(have eaten / ate)* out three times this week.
5. I *(haven't watched / didn't watch)* a good movie for a long time.
6. My friends *(have seen / saw)* a great comedy on Saturday.

UNIT 4

Superlative adjectives: forms and spelling rules

We use superlative adjectives to compare a thing / person (or a group of things / people) to the whole group. The superlative adjective is usually preceded by *the* or a possessive adjective.

- *Rio is **the most exciting** city in the world.*
- *What is **the longest** river in the world?*
- *She's **my best** friend.*
- *This is **our newest** car.*

To form the superlative, we add *-est* to one-syllable adjectives and some two-syllable adjectives.

Spelling rules: short adjectives		
For most one-syllable adjectives, add *the* + *-est.*	*cheap* → ***the cheapest***	*new* → ***the newest***
For short adjectives that end in *-e*, add *the* + *-st.*	*large* → ***the largest***	*fine* → ***the finest***
For short adjectives that end in one vowel and one consonant, double the consonant and add *the* + *-est.*	*big* → ***the biggest***	*fat* → ***the fattest***
For short adjectives that end in a consonant + *-y*, change the *-y* to *-i* and add *the* + *-est.*	*dry* → ***the driest***	*lazy* → ***the laziest***
A few adjectives have an irregular form.	*good* → ***the best***	*bad* → ***the worst***

With most two-syllable adjectives and with longer adjectives, we use *the most* + adjective.

Spelling rules: long adjectives	
famous	***the most famous***
expensive	***the most expensive***

We can leave out the noun if it has already been mentioned.

- *Which city is **the most beautiful**?*
- *Which movie was **the best**?*

NOW PRACTICE

1 Write the superlative form of the adjectives.

1. happy the happiest
2. fat ________
3. amazing ________
4. old ________
5. important ________
6. sad ________
7. cute ________
8. pretty ________
9. bad ________
10. angry ________
11. romantic ________
12. silly ________

2 Complete the questions with the superlative form of the adjective in parentheses.

1. What car is the most expensive? (expensive)
2. What is ________ sport? (dangerous)
3. What is ________ movie you've ever seen? (funny)
4. What kind of music is ________? (relaxing)
5. Who is ________ person in your family? (tall)
6. Who in your family is ________? (thin)

UNIT 5

Adverbial clauses: *before, after,* and *when*

We use the words *before, after,* and *when* to introduce a time clause.

- *I studied English* ***before*** *I went to the United States.*
- *I hope to travel* ***after*** *I finish college.*
- ***When*** *I have a problem, I talk to my friends.*

Time clauses usually follow the main clause, but we can also use them before the main clause. When the time clause comes first, we use a comma (,) to separate it from the main clause.

Main clause	Time clause
He opened his birthday presents	**before** they had dinner.
Everyone watched the fireworks	**after** the stores closed.

Time clause	Main clause
Before they had dinner,	he opened his birthday presents.
After the stores closed,	everyone watched the fireworks.

We use the simple present in a time clause to express future time.

- *I'll be there* ***when*** *the guests* ***arrive****. (~~**I'll be there when the guests will arrive**~~.)*
- ***When*** *classes* ***end****, we're going to go to Spain. (~~**When classes will end, we're going to go to Spain**~~.)*

If both clauses refer to the same period of time, we need to use similar verb forms in each clause.

- *I always* ***listen*** *to music before I* ***go*** *to bed. (~~**I always listen to music before I went to bed**~~.)*
- *Last night I* ***listened*** *to music before I* ***went*** *to bed. (~~**Last night I listened to music before I go to bed**~~.)*

NOW PRACTICE

1 Rewrite these sentences using a time clause with the word in parentheses.

1. I went to Anna's party, and I took a gift. (when)
   When I went to Anna's party, I took a gift.
2. I ate breakfast, and then I went to work. (after)
   ____
3. I was on the bus yesterday, and I fell asleep. (when)
   ____
4. This morning I went jogging, and then I had breakfast. (before)
   ____

2 Complete the sentences with the correct form of the verb in parentheses.

1. When I ___called___ my friend, she didn't answer. (call)
2. She never answers when he __________ her. (call)
3. She'll call you when she __________ home. (get)
4. We left before it __________ to rain. (start)
5. We'll leave when it __________ to rain. (start)
6. It was dark outside when we __________ home this morning. (leave)

UNIT 6

should and *have to*

We often use *should* to ask for and give advice and to make suggestions.

- *What **should** I do to be healthier?*
- *You **should** exercise every day.*
- ***Should** I call her?*

For affirmative statements, we use *should* + the base form of a main verb.

- *We **should** exercise every day.*

For negative statements, we use *should not* or *shouldn't*.

- *They **shouldn't** exercise after eating.*

We use *have to* + the base form of a main verb to talk about obligation and rules.

- *What kinds of clothes **do I have to** wear?*
- ***Does** he **have to** pay for the class?*
- *She **has to** get a job.*
- *You **have to** do more exercise.*

We use *don't have to* when something is not necessary.

- *We **don't have to** wear a uniform to school.*
- *He **doesn't have to** pay for the class.*

NOW PRACTICE

1 Complete the sentences with *should* or *shouldn't* and a verb from the box.

answer drive eat go watch wear

1. It's really cold outside. You _____should wear_____ a coat.
2. You don't look very well. Maybe you ____________________ to the doctor.
3. You ____________________ this movie. It's not very good.
4. The phone's ringing. __________ I __________ it?
5. It's getting late. We ____________________ dinner soon.
6. You ____________________ there. The car isn't working very well.

2 Rewrite the sentences. Use *should, have to,* or *don't have to.*

1. Don't call me. It's not important.
   _____You don't have to call me._____
2. Drink a lot of water. It's a good idea.
   ____
3. Exercise every day. It's a good idea.
   ____
4. Don't tell me again. I understand you.
   ____
5. Take this medicine. It's very important.
   ____

UNIT 7

too / not enough; too many / too much

Too means more than is needed or wanted. We use *too* + an adjective or adverb.

- *It's **too cold**. (= It's colder than I want.)*
- *He eats **too fast**. (= He eats faster than he should.)*

We often use *too* with *many* or *much*. We use *too many* with count nouns and *too much* with noncount nouns.

- *There were **too many people** in the room.*
- *There is **too much water** in the cup.*

Count nouns	Noncount nouns
There are **too many people** in the store. I have **too many books** to read.	They spend **too much money**. We have **too much food**.

We can also use *too much* and *too many* without a noun if the noun was mentioned before or is understood.

- *He doesn't need ten pairs of shoes. He bought **too many**!*
- *She has to work on weekends. That's **too much**! (= too much work)*

Not enough is the opposite of *too*. It means we need or want more of something. We use *not enough* in two ways:

1. *not* + adjective or adverb + *enough*
   - *It's **not** quiet **enough**. (= I want it to be quieter.)*
   - *I ca**n't** run **fast enough**. (= I want to run faster.)*
2. *not enough* + noun
   - *There is**n't enough food**. (= We need more food.)*
   - *I do**n't** have **enough money**. (= I need more money.)*

NOW PRACTICE

1 Complete the sentences with *too much* or *too many*.

1. It's impossible to have ___too much___ jewelry.
2. You can never have ________________ friends.
3. How do you feel when you drink ________________ water?
4. Is it possible to watch ________________ television?
5. Do you spend ________________ hours on the phone?
6. Are there ________________ malls in your area?

2 Complete the sentences. Use *too* or *not enough* and the words in parentheses.

1. Jason wants to buy a car, but he ___doesn't have enough___ money. (have)
2. Ann wants to go to the movies, but she ______________________________ homework. (have / much)
3. Ken wanted to finish his homework, but he ______________________________ time. (have)
4. Erin wanted to see the beginning of the movie, but she ______________________________. (be / late)
5. Linda hoped to pass the test, but she ______________________________. (study / hard)

UNIT 8

Defining relative clauses (subject)

We can use relative clauses to identify, define, or classify a thing or a person.

- *I like people **who are reliable**.*
- *I work at a store **that sells computer games**.*

We use the relative pronouns *who, which*, and *that* to introduce defining relative clauses. *Who* is for people, *which* is for things, *that* is for either people or things.

Main clause	Relative clause	
I like people	**who / that**	are fun.
This is a company	**which / that**	makes computers.

Who, which, and *that* refer back to the thing or person they identify, define, or classify.

- *I have a friend **who** is very polite.*
- *I work at a store **that** sells video games.*

The verb in a subject relative clause agrees in number with the noun in the main clause.

- *I know **a guy** who **speaks** many languages.*
- *I know **some people** who **speak** many languages.*

In a subject relative clause, we don't use a personal subject pronoun after *which, who,* or *that.*

- *I like people who are friendly.* (~~*I like people who they are friendly*~~.)

NOW PRACTICE

1 Complete the sentences with *who* or *which*.

1. I have a car ___which___ is ten years old.
2. There are some students in my class __________ are always late.
3. Do you know anyone __________ is both artistic and reliable?
4. Do you have any books in English __________ are easy to read?
5. Have you ever had a teacher __________ didn't give homework?
6. Have you ever had homework __________ was fun to do?

2 Complete the sentences. Choose the correct form of the verb in parentheses.

1. I have a friend who (*live / lives*) in the US.
2. I have three friends who (*are / is*) already married.
3. My friend plans parties that always (*have / has*) great music.
4. Is there a store around here that (*sell / sells*) electronics?
5. Have you ever had a job that (*were / was*) very interesting?
6. Is there any food that (*make / makes*) you sick?

UNIT 9

The past continuous

We use the past continuous to talk about something in progress at a specific time in the past.

- *In 2008 we* ***were living*** *in Spain.*
- *What* ***were*** *you* ***doing*** *at 10:00 last night?*

We often use the past continuous to talk about something in progress when another action (usually in the simple past) took place.

- *I* ***was making*** *a fire when I* ***burned*** *my hand.*
- *We* ***were watching*** *TV when the lights* ***went*** *out.*

We use the helping verb *be,* not *do,* in past continuous statements and questions.

Affirmative and negative statements			
I / He / She / It	**was sleeping.** **was not reading.** **wasn't reading.**	You / We / They	**were reading.** **were not sleeping.** **weren't sleeping.**

Wh- questions							
Where	**was**	I / he / she / it	**sleeping?**	Where	**were**	you / we / they	**sleeping?**

NOW PRACTICE

1 Complete the sentences with the verb in parentheses. Use the past continuous or simple past form.

1. He ____lost____ a tooth while he was playing football. (lose)
2. She ________________ a motorcycle when she had the accident. (ride)
3. We were really bored when we ________________ the movie. (watch)
4. I ________________at the gym when you called. (exercise)
5. He was running when he ________________ down the stairs. (fall)

2 Answer the questions with information about you.

1. What were you doing at 9:00 yesterday morning?

   ____

2. Where were you studying when you first took an English class?

   ____

3. Where were your parents living when they met?

   ____

4. What was your teacher doing when you started class today?

   ____

UNIT 10

used to: statements and questions

We use *used to* + the base form of a verb for past habits or situations that are different now.

- *They **used to play** soccer, but they don't anymore.*
- *I **used to take** the bus to school, but now I drive.*
- *That building **used to be** a school, but it's a store now.*

Affirmative statements			
I / You / He / She / It / We / They	**used to**	**live**	in Australia.

We use *didn't* + *use to* in negative statements. We use *did* + *use to* in questions.

- *I **didn't use to like** singing. (I **didn't ~~used~~ to like** singing.)*
- *Where **did you use to live**? (Where **did you ~~used~~ to live?**)*
- ***Did he use to play** an instrument? (**Did he ~~used~~ to play** an instrument?)*

Negative statements			
I / You / He / She / It / We / They	**didn't use to**	**live**	in Australia.

Wh- questions				
Where	**did**	I / you / he / she / it / we / they	**use to**	**live**?

It is common to use *never used to* as a negative form.

- *I **never used to like** country music, but now I love it.*

NOW PRACTICE

1 Complete the sentences with *used to* or *didn't use to*.

1. People __didn't use to__ write emails. They wrote letters instead.
2. Men ______________ wear hats all the time, but now they don't.
3. People ______________ watch TV at home, but now they can watch it in different places.
4. Children ______________ have a lot of free time to play. They had to work instead.
5. People ______________ get married at a younger age.

2 Complete the conversations. Use the verb in parentheses.

1. **A** How do you like it here?
   B It's nice, but I'm a little homesick.
   A Where __did you use to live__ (live) ?
   B In Costa Rica.
2. **A** How long have you been a chef?
   B For about six months.
   A Really? What ______________________ (do) ?
   B I was a dancer.
3. **A** What do you think of your teacher?
   B She's a good teacher, but she's very serious.
   A Yeah, she ______________________ (be) like that. She used to be fun.

UNIT 11

If clauses with zero conditional

We use the zero conditional to talk about events and results that are always true. We use the simple present in the *if* clause and the simple present in the result clause.

- *If you **click** on the link, the website **comes up**.*
- *If you **don't bring** your reusable bag, you **pay** for another one.*

If clauses with first conditional and *may / might*

We use the first conditional for possible events in the future when one event depends on another. We use the simple present in the *if* clause. We use *will, may,* or *might* + the base form of a verb in the main clause.

- *If you **stop** using the electric heater every day, you **will save** money.*
- *If we only **shop** at the superstore, local stores **might close**.*

The *if* clause can come before or after the main clause. When the *if* clause comes first, we use a comma (,) after it.

- ***If I go to Japan**, I'll visit Kyoto and Nara.*
- *I might take a taxi home **if I work late tonight**.*

***Yes / No* questions**	
Will you stop using a plastic bag	if I **give** you a reusable one?

***Wh-* questions**	
Where **will you live**	if you **move** to the city?
How **will you travel**	if you **go** on vacation this year?
Which bus **will you take**	if you **get** a job downtown?

We can use affirmative or negative verbs in one clause or in both clauses.

- *If I **move** apartments, I'**ll recycle** my old desk and chair.*
- *If I **get** a job, I **won't have** time to go to the gym.*
- *If I **don't get** a job, I **might not** have enough money for the gym membership.*

NOW PRACTICE

1 Complete the questions and statements. Choose the correct verb form.

1. If you don't study for the test next week, what (*might happen / happens*)?
2. How (*will you come / do you come*) to work if you move to a farm?
3. What will you do if you (*won't find / don't find*) a good job?
4. If you (*will be / are*) late to class, what will your teacher say?
5. He always gives me a plastic straw if I (*order / will order*) a milkshake!
6. If people don't use their cars, they (*might reduce / won't reduce*) pollution.

2 Complete the sentences with the correct form of the verb in parentheses.

1. If he __doesn't call__ me tonight, I won't speak to him again. (call)
2. You ____________ waste if you take your reusable cup to the coffee shop. (reduce)
3. You might get hurt if you ____________ . (slow down)
4. If you go to the secondhand store, you ____________ money. (save)
5. ____________ you ____________ your jeans to charity if you buy some new ones? (give)

UNIT 12

Modals for possibility, speculation, and deduction

We use *may*, *might*, or *could* + base form to talk about possibility in the present and future.

- *Your phone* ***could be*** *in your bag.* (about the present)
- *It* ***may rain*** *later, so bring your coat.* (about the future)
- *He* ***might not be*** *ready to take his driving test.* (about the present)
- *We* ***might paint*** *the walls a different color.* (about the future)

We also use *may (not)*, *might (not)*, *could (not)*, *can't*, *must (not)* to express degrees of certainty when we speculate about (or offer reasons to explain) different people or situations, or deduce something (make conclusions) using information available to us.

- *I saw her going into her house. She* ***must be*** *at home. (= I'm almost 100% sure it is true.)*
- *Their car isn't on the street. They* ***must not be*** *at home. (= I'm 75% sure it is true.)*
- *She speaks Portuguese. She* ***might be*** *from Brazil. (= I'm not sure if it is true.)*
- *I just saw him in the park. He* ***can't be*** *in the library. (= I'm almost 100% sure it is not true.)*

Notice the difference between *may not / might not* and *can't*:

- *He* ***may / might not be*** *at home. (= It is possible that he is not at home. I'm not sure.)*
- *He* ***can't be*** *at home. I just saw him in the park. (= It is not possible that he is at home.)*

Must not is sometimes used when the speaker is almost certain.

- *The lights are off. They* ***must not be*** *at home.*

NOW PRACTICE

1 Read each sentence. Then choose the best sentence to follow it.

1. You're so good with people.
   a. You could be a student.
   b. You could get a job as a tour guide.
2. She speaks Japanese.
   a. She must be from Japan.
   b. She may be from Japan.
3. Jay is good at math.
   a. He might major in engineering.
   b. He can't major in engineering.
4. My keys are always at the office.
   a. They can't be at home.
   b. They might be at home.

2 Complete the conversations. Choose the correct answer.

1. A This project looks interesting. I want to do volunteering after I graduate.
   B Good idea. It's all about wildlife, so you (*must / might*) work with animals.
   A Great. Where's the project?
   B I guess you (*could / can't*) do it anywhere animals are in danger.
2. A Why isn't Sarah here?
   B I don't know. She (*might / must*) be sick.
   A She (*might not / can't*) be. I just saw her jogging.
3. A Where is everyone? All the classrooms are empty.
   B Everyone (*can't / might not*) be late.
   A No, we (*must not / might*) have any classes today!

AUDIO SCRIPTS

UNIT 1 LISTENING p. 7

T=Tim J=Jane

T Hi, Jane!
J Hi, Tim! Great to see you!
T Great to see you, too. Did you have a good vacation?
J Yes, I did!
T So did I. What did you do?
J I went to Europe.
T Really? That's awesome. Where did you go?
J Italy. Florence.
T Nice place for a vacation.
J Actually it wasn't really a vacation. I went to art classes.
T Really? Were they good?
J Yes. I learned a lot about art. And I also learned some Italian.
T Do you want to study art this semester?
J No. I want to study languages.
T Ah! So do I.
J I want to study Italian and Portuguese. What about you?
T I want to study Chinese. One of my grandmothers is Chinese.
J Really? I didn't know that. So, what did YOU do on the vacation? Did you get to travel any place?
T Not really. I visited my grandparents in San Francisco.
J Oh! Your grandparents live in San Francisco?
T Yes.
J So do mine!
T Actually, I visited them because I did a summer school program in San Francisco.
J Really? What kind of program?
T Acting class.
J No kidding! You went to acting classes?
T Yes.
J Were they fun?
T Yes! But they were hard work.
J So were my art classes in Florence!
T We worked ten hours a day.
J So did we!
T At the end, we put on a show at the Comedy Theater.
J Wow. That's impressive.
T I think we both worked hard during the vacation.
J Yes, I think we did.

LISTENING PLUS

L=Lisa J=Jane

L Jane! Hi!
J Hey, Lisa! Hello!
L How are you?
J I'm fine. Lisa, this is my friend Tim.
L Pleased to meet you, Tim.
T Pleased to meet you too, Lisa.
L Actually, I think I know you from someplace.
T Really?
J Yes. Weren't you in my Portuguese class last semester?
T No, I didn't study Portuguese.
L OK ... So, Jane, how was your vacation?
J Great. I went to Italy again.
L Oh, how cool! We met there last year, remember?
J Of course I remember!
L You're so lucky. I didn't get a chance to travel.
J Nor did Tim.
L Really? What did you do, Tim?
T I went to San Francisco.
L Really? So did I! I went to visit my grandparents.
T So did I!
J But he also did acting classes!
L No way!
J And at the end, they did a show.
L Really? Where did you do it?
T At the Comedy Theater.
L Ah! I think that's where I saw you.
T You were there?
L Yes, I was.
T No way.
L And you were very good!

UNIT 2 LISTENING p. 13

1 H=Host S=Sandra

H Welcome to the *Free Time Show*. I have some very interesting young people with me today. So let's meet the first one. Hello, what's your name and how old are you?
S My name is Sandra Hancox and I'm 18 years old.
H And you have an interesting free-time activity, right?
S Right.
H What is it you like to do?
S I like to make horror movies.
H Horror movies? Do you like to act in them or to direct them?
S I like to direct, and my friends are the actors.
H Do your friends enjoy acting in them?
S Yes, they do. They think it's really exciting.
H And where do you usually make these movies?
S Oh, you know, in friends' houses and apartments. And, occasionally, in small studios.
H But next week you're going to do something different, right?
S Yes, we're going to make a movie in a beach house, with monsters coming from the sea.
H That's very cool. When you finish, can you come back and tell us about it?
S Sure!

2 H=Host A=Alison

H And my next guest is Alison Sutton. Hi, Alison. Welcome to the show.
A Thank you.
H Now, Alison. You're friends with my last guest, Sandra, is that right?
A Right.
H And you're going to do something together?
A Yes, we are. Sandra wants to make a horror movie in a beach house.
H A movie with monsters coming out of the sea, right?
A Yes!
H So tell me about the monster. Is it really big?
A Well, actually, you don't see the complete monster. Just its head and mouth. But it's really frightening.

H I see. And what's your part in the movie?
A I play a local police officer.
H Oh, so you aren't the victim of the monster?
A No, the victim is a man.
H Interesting! And what happens?
A I can't tell you that. It's a secret.
H Oh OK. Now I'm really interested!
A Good!
H Can you come back with Sandra and tell us about it?
A I'd love to.

3 **H**=Host **A**=Andy

H My next guest is Andy Newman. Welcome to the show, Andy.
A Thank you.
H How old are you, Andy?
A I'm 18 years old.
H And you're a very talented musician, right?
A Um, I guess. I can play a few instruments.
H What can you play?
A Piano, guitar, and I'm going to learn to play the violin.
H I'm impressed. So, do you want to play in an orchestra?
A Well, yes, one day. But right now, I'm playing guitar in a rock band.
H Really?
A Yes, my ambition is to tour with a really famous band.
H Right, and I understand that you're doing something about that soon, right?
A That's right. Next week my favorite band is in town, and we're going to open for them—you know, play before they start.
H That's great! Come back and tell us how it goes, OK?
A Sure!

4 **H**=Host **B**=Briana **E**=Enrique

H And now I have two very nice young people with me. Hi. What are your names, and how old are you?
B I'm Briana Lopez and I'm 19, and this is my brother Enrique. He's 18.
E Hi.
H And what do you do in your free time?
B We write songs.
H What kind of songs?
E All kinds—blues, country, pop.
H Do you write the songs together?
E We write the words together, but then I usually write the music myself.
H Do you both sing and play instruments?
B I sing and Enrique plays the keyboard.
H And do you record them?
B Well, we already recorded some of them on a computer, but next week, we're going to a real studio.
E We have the chance to record five of our favorite songs.
H Oh, that's very exciting. Well, please come back and tell us all about it.
B We'd love to.

LISTENING PLUS

H=Host **S**=Sandra **A**=Alison **An**=Andy **B**=Briana **E**=Enrique

H Ladies and gentlemen, please welcome my guests, Sandra Hancox and Alison Sutton! Welcome back!
S Thank you. Nice to be here.
A Hello again.
H So, Sandra, did you make your horror movie in the beach house?
S Yes, we did.
H And how was it?
S Awesome! It was a very interesting experience.
H Alison, did the actors enjoy it, too?
A Yes, they did. They were all very excited about it.
H Did you have any problems?
S Actually, we did—with one of the scenes.
H OK ... What happened?
S Well, in this scene two of the actors run on the beach and start screaming.
H Right? ...
S Well, someone on the beach got scared and called the police.
H Oh, no!
S Oh, yes ... And suddenly there were police cars everywhere.
A Yes, they were a little surprised when they saw me, because I was in a police uniform.
H Oh, right! Did you explain about the movie?
A Yes, we did.
H And what happened.
S The police were OK about it.
H And did you finish the movie?
S Yes, we did.
H Are you happy with it?
S Yes, it was a really exciting experience.
H What about you, Alison?
A It was great but I want to do it again. I want to be better!
H Hello, Andy. Welcome back.
An Thank you.
H Did you get to open for your favorite band?
An Yes.
H How did it go?
An I was a little disappointed.
H Why? Wasn't the concert good?
An Oh, no, the concert was amazing. I was disappointed with myself. My performance was terrible.
H Well, it was a good experience, right?
An Yes. I just want to do it again and get it right.
H Best of luck!
An Thank you.
H Hi, Briana and Enrique. Welcome back.
B/E Thank you.
H Good to see you again. Did you go to the recording studio?
B Yes, we did.
H How was it?
B Amazing.
E Awesome.
B The studio people were so good. Really helpful.
H How many songs did you record?
B Only three. That was the only problem.
E Yep, we didn't have enough time.
H Well, I hope you get another chance.
B So do we!
H Good luck!
B/E Thank you!

UNIT 3 LISTENING p. 19

M=Marco A=Anya

M Hello?
A Hey, Marco, what's up?
M Oh, hi, Anya.
A How are you?
M Oh ... OK, I guess.
A Hey, you don't sound too good. What's the problem?
M I'm filling out an application.
A What kind of application?
M To be a counselor at a summer camp.
A Oh, OK. So, what's the problem?
M I'm having trouble with one of the questions.
A What's the question?
M "Have you ever done anything interesting or unusual?"
A Uh, OK. Well, have you?
M I'm not sure.
A Well, uh, have you ever traveled to any unusual places?
M Um ... I've been to Mexico. But I guess a lot of people have been to Mexico, right?
A Yes, you're right. Have you been to any other place outside the US?
M No, I haven't.
A OK ... Have you ... um ... have you done any extreme sports, like skydiving?
M Um ... well, I went whitewater rafting once.
A Oh, excellent! Where did you do that?
M In Colorado. I was there for my 18th birthday, just last month.
A OK, so write that down.
M And we went snowboarding when I was there, too.
A Snowboarding in Colorado! Write it down.
M Oh, I almost forgot! I went cave diving in Florida once.
A Cave diving? Wow. I'd love to try cave diving someday. How was it?
M Oh, I can't really remember. It was years ago.
A Did you go on your own?
M No, I went with my parents. I think I was about 10 or so ...
A Cool. Anyway, you see? You've done lots of exciting stuff! Write it all down and send the application.

LISTENING PLUS

A=Anya M=Marco

A Hello?
M Hi, Anya. It's Marco.
A Hey, Marco. How are you?
M OK, I guess.
A Have you sent the application?
M Yes, I have.
A Have you gotten a reply?
M Yes, I have.
A And ... ?
M I got the camp counselor's job.
A Great!
M There's just one problem. Well, two actually.
A Uh-huh?
M I have to teach the kids how to swim.
A Oh. And what's the problem? You can't swim?
M Of course I can swim!
A So what's the problem?
M I don't go swimming very often. I'm out of practice.
A How long before you start at the summer camp?
M Three months.
A Well, then find a swimming pool and practice again.
M OK.
A Every day!
M I'll try.
A OK, so try! What's the other problem?
M I need a driver's license.
A And you don't have one?
M No, I don't. I failed my test.
A Come on. You have three months! You can take the test again and pass it!
M Anya ...
A Yes?
M I love your confidence!

UNIT 4 LISTENING p. 27

H=Host J=Jose S=Seiko A=Amy T=Tony

H Good evening everyone and welcome to *The College Quiz Show*! And tonight, our two teams are from Washington College and San Francisco College. So please welcome Jose and Amy from Washington College! And from San Francisco, please welcome Seiko and Tony! OK, the rules are simple. In round one, there are five questions and anyone can answer. You just hit the buzzer. If you're wrong, the other team can answer. Two points for a correct answer, and the questions are about continents. So, let's get started. Question one: Which is the biggest continent in the world? Jose?
J Asia.
H That is correct! Two points! Asia is the biggest continent. It also has a bigger population than any other continent—over four billion people or about 60 percent of the population of the entire world. So, what is the second largest continent in the world? Seiko?
S North America?
H No, Seiko, I'm sorry, that's wrong. Amy?
A Africa?
H Yes! Africa is the second largest continent. There are more than 50 countries in Africa. Imagine that! For an extra two points: the world's biggest subtropical desert is in Africa. Can you name it? Tony?
T The biggest subtropical desert is ... the Sahara?
H Right! Two points! OK. Question three: Which is the smallest continent? Amy?
A Europe?
H No, Amy, that's wrong. Tony?
T Australia.
H That's right! Two points! OK. Question four: Does anyone know which continent has the fewest people? Amy?
A Antarctica?
H That's right. Now, North America consists of three large countries—Canada, the US, and Mexico. So, question five—the last question in this round: What is ... the largest city in North America? Seiko?
S Mexico City?
H Correct! Mexico City has a population of around 22 million people in its metropolitan area. By the way, the name of every continent begins and ends with the letter *A*, except one—Europe. So, the scores at the end of round one are ...

LISTENING PLUS

H=Host S=Seiko T=Tony A=Amy J=Jose

H So, the scores at the end of round one are ... Washington College has six points and San Francisco College has six points! OK, teams, in round two, you choose a number from one to six, and you answer a question on the subject of that number. So, San Francisco, give me a number between one and six.

S Five.

H Number five. Your question will be on ... rivers. OK, here's your question. What is the longest river in the world?

S Uh ... Well, I guess the answer is the Nile? I mean, the Amazon is really long, too ...

T I think it's the Amazon.

S You do? OK. We'll say the Amazon. Is it the Amazon?

H No, it isn't. And I can give the question to Washington College.

A I think it's the Nile, too. What do you think?

J I think it's the Mississippi.

A The Mississippi?

J Yes.

A OK. Is it the Mississippi?

H No! It's the Nile. OK, Washington College, give me a number.

J One.

H Your question is on ... mountains. The Himalayas mountain range is in five different countries. Three of those countries are China, Bhutan, and Nepal. What are the other two countries?

A We don't know, sorry.

H San Francisco, do you want to try?

T Russia and Afghanistan?

H No, Tony, you're way off. The answer is India and Pakistan. OK. The scores are even, so I have one final question for both teams. Back on the buzzers. The tallest mountains in the world are in the Himalayas, but where is the tallest mountain outside the Himalayas? Amy?

A Kilimanjaro? In Africa?

H No, I'm afraid it isn't. Does anyone else want to try? OK, well, the answer is Aconcagua, and it's nearly 7,000 meters tall. So, still no winner. Back on the buzzers. Does anyone want to take a guess where Aconcagua is? Tony?

T South America?

H Yes! Where?

A Um ... Argentina?

H ... is the right answer! So, San Francisco College is tonight's winner!

UNIT 5 LISTENING p. 33

1 I=Interviewer B=Brendan

I Brendan, tell me about New Year's in Ireland.

B Well, first of all, it's very important that you clean your house before the end of the year. Your house must be really clean before the new year starts.

I I see. Anything else?

B It's also lucky if the first person to come into your house after midnight is a tall, dark, handsome man. And he must go in the front door and go out the back door.

I Interesting.

B Very good if it's a tall, dark, handsome man. Not very good if it's a red-haired woman.

I It isn't good if a woman with red hair comes into the house?

B If she's the first one, it's not good. If she comes in after the tall, dark, handsome man, then it's OK.

I Brendan, you're tall, dark, and handsome.

B Oh, thank you.

I Do people ask you to be the first person in their house?

B Actually, yes, they do.

I I'm not surprised.

B Oh, there's one other thing. If you're single and you want to get married in the new year, you put some mistletoe under your pillow.

I Under your pillow?

B Right. That way, when you go to sleep, you dream about your future husband or wife.

I Are you single, Brendan?

B Yes, I am, actually ...

2 I=Interviewer Y=Yang-hee

I Yang-hee, what happens on New Year's Eve in Korea?

Y Oh, I love our New Year's Eve festival—we call it *Seotdal Geumeum*. It's the night when no one sleeps. In the past, some people believed that if you sleep that night, your eyebrows turn white!

I Your eyebrows turn white?

Y Yes! And to make sure this doesn't happen, we leave the lights on in every room of the house.

I Interesting.

Y New Year's is also a nice time for children. On New Year's Day, they get a lucky bag from their parents or grandparents.

I A lucky bag?

Y Yes. We call them *bokjumeoni*. They're made of silk—very beautiful!

I What's in the lucky bags?

Y Usually money, but sometimes other small gifts, too.

3 I=Interviewer A=Andrea

I Andrea, tell me about New Year's in Brazil.

A Well, the best place to be on New Year's is at the beach.

I I'm sure it is.

A And the first thing to know is this: you have to wear white clothes.

I So everyone is on the beach wearing white clothes?

A Yes, and everyone has white flowers. And you must make sure that your right foot is on the floor when the clock strikes midnight.

I I see. And then what happens?

A First we throw the flowers onto the beach, and then we walk into the water.

I In your white clothes?

A Correct. And we have to jump over seven waves.

I I see.

A And after we come out of the water, we eat seven grapes.

I OK. That's a lot of things to remember!

LISTENING PLUS

I=Interviewer B=Brendan Y=Yang-hee A=Andrea

I Brendan, have you ever spent New Year's in another country?

B Oh, yes, last year—in Australia.

I Tell me about it.

B I went to visit my brother. He lives in Sydney. Some of his friends invited us to their apartment. There was a wonderful view of the Opera House. Have you ever seen a picture of the Sydney Opera House?

I Oh, yes, it's beautiful. So, how was the party?
B Actually, the party was quiet—dinner with about 10 people. When the party started, my brother's friend said, "We have someone here from Ireland. That's very lucky!"
I That's nice! So, what happened at midnight?
B Well, half an hour before midnight, we all walked down to the waterfront to look at the Sydney Harbor Bridge. At midnight, there was a fireworks display there.
I Was it good?
B It was magnificent. After the fireworks finished, there was a big street party.
I So, how would you describe New Year's in Sydney?
B Unforgettable!
I Yang-hee, have you ever spent New Year's outside Korea?
Y Yes, two years ago, when I visited my cousin in San Francisco.
I What did you do?
Y Well, my cousin made a really nice Korean meal. After we ate it, we went out. We went down to the dock and went on a boat cruise.
I A boat cruise?
Y Yes, we took a cruise around San Francisco Bay. When the boat reached the Golden Gate Bridge, a fireworks display started. It was really amazing!
I So you enjoyed New Year's in San Francisco.
Y Oh, yes! It was magic!
I Andrea, have you ever spent New Year's in any place other than Brazil?
A Yes. About ten years ago, I studied English in London, England, and I spent New Year's there.
I What did you do?
A Well, I went to a party with an English friend. I brought a lot of grapes, and I wanted to do the Brazilian thing—you know, eat seven grapes? But no one wanted to do it.
I Why not?
A Because they wanted to watch TV.
I Why?
A They wanted to watch the New Year fireworks.
I Were the fireworks good?
A Yes, but they were on TV! Fireworks are not exciting on TV.
I Then what happened?
A After the fireworks, everyone went home.
I So, what word describes your New Year's in London?
A Disappointing.

UNIT 6 LISTENING p. 39

H=Health expert B=Brian E=Erin

H Hello!
B Hi.
H Can I help you?
B Uh ... I don't know. Maybe you can give me some advice.
H Sure. Do you want to take a seat? So, what's your name?
B Brian.
H And how old are you, Brian?
B I'm 52.
H OK. What do you do?
B I work with computers.
H So you spend a lot of time in front of a computer?
B Yeah, usually. It depends, but some days, 12 hours.
H Wow, that's a long time. Do you have to work that long?
B Well, I don't have to, but I do. I like my work. Is that bad?
H Well, it's good that you like your work, but 12 hours is a lot. How do you get to work? Do you walk? Take the bus?
B No, I have to drive.
H You have to drive?
B There isn't a bus or a subway from where I live.
H Really?
B Well, there is a bus, but it's a 15-minute walk from my apartment.
H I see.
B Should I stop driving to work?
H Well, maybe you shouldn't drive all the time. Maybe you should take the bus two or three times a week. Walking to the bus is good exercise, and I think you need that.
B OK.
H Do you go to the gym?
B Not anymore. But I do play ping pong once in a while.
H OK, that's not bad, but it's not enough exercise. You should do more than that.
B Right.
H What about food? What kind of food do you eat?
B I eat a lot of pizza. Maybe four or five times a week.
H Do you eat any vegetables or fruit?
B Oh, yes, I eat salad—maybe once a month.
H OK. Well, this is my advice: you really should walk and get some exercise. And you shouldn't eat so much pizza! You should eat more fruit and vegetables, and cook more fresh food.
B OK, I'll try.
E Hi, my name's Erin.
H Nice to meet you, Erin. How can I help you?
E I think I need to change my lifestyle.
H OK. How old are you?
E 26.
H And what do you do?
E I'm a teacher.
H Do you enjoy your work?
E Yes, I like it, but I get stressed a lot, and I'm always tired.
H Do you exercise?
E Well, I ride my bike everywhere.
H That's good. And what do you do to relax?
E Um ... I watch TV ...
H Well, that's OK, but if you get stressed a lot, maybe you should try something like meditation or tai chi.
E Really? Do meditation and tai chi help?
H They're very good for a lot of people. You should try it.
E OK.
H And what kinds of things do you like to eat?
E I like all kinds of food, but I live alone and don't have much time to cook.
H So, what do you eat?
E Fast food, most days, and I drink a lot of soda.
H Ah ... OK. Well, Erin, first of all, you should try to cook fresh food more often. It really doesn't take that much time. And if you eat fast food, you should try to eat some salad with it.
E OK.
H And my advice is: drink less soda.
E Less soda. OK.
H In fact, you should stop drinking it completely.
E Stop drinking soda? What should I drink, then?

H Try drinking more water and herbal tea. Actually, they have a great herbal tea at the stand over there. You should try some.
E OK. Thanks.

LISTENING PLUS

E=Erin B=Brian

E Hi.
B Hello?
E Can I join you?
B Uh ... do we know each other?
E No, but you talked to the Healthier Life lady, right?
B Yes.
E So did I.
B Oh, really?
E So, can I join you?
B Sure.
E Thanks. Your name is Brian, right?
B Yes. And you are ... ?
E Erin.
B Nice to meet you, Erin. What's that you're drinking?
E This? Oh, it's herbal tea.
B Ugh ...
E It's good, actually! I'm changing my life, and this is the start. Is that soda?
B Yes, it is.
E I drink a lot of soda.
B Me, too.
E You do? Well, we should both drink less soda.
B I agree.
E In fact, we should stop drinking soda completely.
B Well, I'm not so sure about that.
E Well, I'm going to stop drinking soda starting today. What's that you're eating?
B It's just a cookie.
E It's a big cookie. And it's chocolate, right?
B Yeah.
E Maybe you should stop eating cookies, too.
B Well, maybe ...
E Another thing—and I'm sorry if this is a personal question, Brian, but—do you exercise at all?
B Exercise? Sure I do.
E Great! What do you do?
B Well, every morning, I walk to my car.
E You walk to your car? Brian, walking to your car is not exercise!
B Listen, Erin—I live in an apartment, and I have to park my car a long way from it.
E How far?
B About a half mile. I have to walk to the car in the morning, and I have to walk back to my apartment in the evening. That's a mile.
E Do you go the gym?
B Not anymore.
E Why not?
B It's too far away.
E How far?
B About two miles. And there's no place to park my car.
E Why don't you walk there?
B Walk two miles? Are you crazy?
E You don't have to do it every day.
B Erin, you sure have some crazy ideas.
E Yes, Brian, but it's time to change. We both have to change our lifestyles!
B Yes, but maybe we shouldn't change too fast, eh?

UNIT 7 LISTENING p. 47

1 I=Interviewer J=James

I Excuse me. I'm doing a survey about shopping habits. Can I ask you a few questions?
J Sure.
I Can I have your name?
J James Golding.
I OK, James, question one: Do you like shopping at malls?
J Yes, I love going to malls. There's a great mall near my place. It's very convenient.
I What do you like about it?
J Well, there are so many stores.
I OK. Anything you don't like?
J Well, sometimes there are too many people. And I never have enough time.
I Next, do you like shopping alone or with friends?
J Oh, with friends! Always!
I What about shopping online? Do you like it?
J No, I don't. I very rarely shop online.
I Why not?
J I'm not happy about giving personal information online—you know, your credit card number, that kind of thing.
I But it's really safe these days.
J Maybe, but I still prefer real stores!

2 I=Interviewer S=Sofia

I Excuse me. I'm doing a survey about shopping habits. Can I ask you some questions?
S OK.
I What's your name?
S Sofia.
I Tell me, Sofia, do you like shopping at malls?
S No! I hate it!
I Really? Why?
S There are too many stores, there are too many people, and there's too much noise! Shopping at a mall is very stressful!
I OK. Next question: Do you like shopping alone or with friends?
S Well, if I have to go to stores, I prefer to shop alone. But really, I prefer to buy stuff online.
I What kinds of things do you buy online?
S Everything—electronics, clothing ... I even bought my bicycle online.
I Are there any problems with shopping online?
S Yes, sometimes, if you don't want something, it's too difficult to send it back.
I Don't you think it's dangerous to give your credit card information?
S Yeah, that's a good point. I didn't think it was dangerous, but then a friend of mine had a problem. Someone got his credit card details and spent a lot of money with his card. So, yes, it's a little dangerous, but you can find good stuff there.

3 I=Interviewer G=Goku

I Excuse me. I'm doing a survey about shopping habits. Can I ask you some questions?
G Sure. What do you want to know?
I OK, first of all, what's your name?

G Goku Suzuki. You can call me Gok.
I Thanks. So, Gok, do you like shopping at malls?
G Yes, I do.
I What do you like about it?
G Well, you can find everything you want there—under one roof.
I Is there anything you don't like about malls?
G Well, there are too many places to go, and I never have enough time.
I Do you like to shop with friends or alone?
G Both. I like to shop alone and with friends.
I OK. What about shopping online?
G Oh, I love it! I buy a lot of things online. Actually, my best friend thinks I buy too much stuff online!
I What's the best thing about shopping online?
G The choices! And you can see them all without leaving home.
I How do you know if things you see online are good?
G I always read the customer reviews. They're usually pretty reliable.
I Any problems with online shopping?
G Yes! Online shopping is too tempting. It's very easy to spend too much money online.
I Do you think it's dangerous to shop online?
G Dangerous? No, not at all.

LISTENING PLUS

I=Interviewer **G**=Gok **S**=Sofia

I Hello again. I'm with Gok and Sofia, and we're talking some more about shopping. Gok, what kind of shopping do you like to do?
G Well, like I said, I love going to the mall. We have a great one here.
I Sofia?
S I hate going to the mall. The mall in this town is too big, and there are always too many people there.
G But that's not a problem. You can take a break. Don't you like just sitting, having coffee, and people-watching?
S Coffee is fine, but people-watching—no way.
I Sofia, you prefer shopping online, right?
S Right. It's easy; it's quick. You can look at stuff. You can take your time and think ...
G But you can do that at the mall, too.
S No, you can't! You stop, you look at something, and a store assistant says, "Hi! Can I help you?" I don't like it.
G Right. And you say, "No, thank you, just looking." It's easy.
I So, Gok, you said you buy a lot of things online?
G Yes, I buy things all the time. Stuff like books and tickets for shows ... But I never buy clothes or shoes. I mean, imagine buying a pair of shoes online. That's just crazy.
S Why?
G Because you have to see them, try them on. See if they're the right size.
S That isn't a problem. If you buy something online and you don't like it, you can send it back.
I So, Sofia, aren't you going to change your mind about shopping in malls?
S I don't think so.
I How about if Gok takes you mall shopping?
S What?
G Sure thing!
S Hold on a second.
I So, this is the challenge: Gok is going to take Sofia shopping at the mall. We're going to see if she can change her mind about it. OK, you guys?
G Yes! Come on, Sofia! We're going to have a great time.
S I am not so sure about that.

UNIT 8 LISTENING p. 53

1 Hi, Connie. My name is Anita, and my husband and I live in California. We're planning to do a road trip across the US starting in September. We want to drive across four states, and visit friends and family on the way, so we're looking for someone who can house-sit for us for six months, until next March. We don't actually have any animals, and we have a cleaner who comes every week. She's a really nice woman, but she isn't very reliable. Sometimes she doesn't come for two or three weeks, so we're looking for someone who can do all those things—clean the house and buy stuff. What do you think?

2 Hello, Connie. I'm Chuck, and I live in Montana. I need someone to look after my house during July and August. I'm going to be in Europe during that time. Good to know that you like animals. Do you know anything about horses? I have three horses that need a lot of attention. They're all quite energetic. Just one thing, the house is about five miles from the nearest town. I saw that you don't have a driver's license, but I have a motorcycle that you can use. Is that OK?

3 Hello Connie. My name is Lucy, and my mother and I live in Santa Fe, New Mexico. We're planning to go to Bolivia in July to work for a charity. We're looking for someone who can live in our house while we're away. We have dogs and cats and also a lot of tropical fish. Do you know anything about looking after fish? It's all pretty simple. And the dogs are really lovely, quiet, well behaved, fun to be with. One of the cats is a little crazy, but she's isn't a problem most of the time. We live about a mile from the nearest shopping mall. There isn't a bus, but we have bicycles. Would you like us to call you for a chat?

LISTENING PLUS

L=Lucy **C**=Connie

L Hello, Lucy Barron speaking.
C Hi, Lucy, this is Connie Watson.
L I'm sorry, Connie who?
C I'm the person who wants to house-sit for you?
L Oh, Connie! Sorry, yes. Nice to hear from you.
C Thank you. Is it OK if I ask a few questions?
L Sure. What would you like to know?
C Well, first of all, you said you had dogs and cats, right?
L Right.
C How many?
L How many dogs and cats?
C Yes.
L Just the one dog. Her name is Lucy, too.
C OK. And how many cats?
L I'm not sure.
C I'm sorry?
L I'm not sure. My mom is someone who really likes cats. She finds them mostly at the mall.
C So there are a lot of cats.
L Right.
C About how many?
L I don't know. Twelve, maybe. Fourteen?

C Wow, that's a lot of cats!
L Yeah, but really they aren't a problem. They sleep most of the time.
C And there are also fish?
L Right. Tropical fish. About a hundred of them
C A hundred?
L Yes, but there's a very good website with information about them.
C A website? I need to go on a website to look after them?
L Yes. I've made some notes about the ones that need special attention.
C I see. And you say your house is about a mile from the shopping mall?
L Maybe a little more.
C More than a mile?
L Yes, maybe three or four miles.
C OK. Is there a bus that goes there from your neighborhood?
L No, not really. Well, there IS a bus, but it doesn't go near the house.
C I see. Well, thank you very much. It's been interesting talking to you.

UNIT 9 LISTENING p. 59

1 **F**=Friend **A**=Ana
F What did you do on your vacation last year, Ana?
A I went jet-skiing. It was my first time.
F Oh? Did you have a good time?
A Actually, no. I broke my arm.
F Oh, no! Jet-skiing is so dangerous!
A I didn't break my arm when I was jet-skiing.
F No?
A No. I broke it in the bathroom of my hotel room.
F Really? How did you do that?
A I fell while I was getting out of the shower.
F Oh! That's too bad.

2 **F**=Friend **M**=Max
F Where did you go on vacation last year, Max?
M Nowhere. I stayed at home.
F Oh well, relaxing at home can be good.
M I didn't plan to stay home. I planned to go waterskiing in Florida.
F Oh, I see. So why didn't you go?
M Because I sprained my wrist.
F How did you do that?
M I was cleaning the windows, and I fell off a ladder.
F Oh, too bad!
M My dad was really upset.
F Really?
M Yes. He was sitting near the ladder, and I fell on top of him!

3 **F**=Friend **A**=Amy
F What did you do on vacation last year, Amy?
A I went canoeing at Yellowstone.
F Nice! Did you enjoy it?
A Um ... well, I enjoyed the vacation, but I cut my knee pretty badly.
F Uh-oh. I guess canoeing can be dangerous, huh?
A Actually, I didn't cut my knee while I was canoeing.
F No?
A No. I did it while I was taking my canoe up a hill.
F Huh? What happened?
A I wasn't looking where I was going, and I tripped over a rock.
F Terrible!
A It was. But then my instructor helped me. In fact, he carried me up the hill and then drove me to the hospital.
F Good.
A Yes, very good. He was a very nice guy.
F And ... ?
A And, well, let's say I know him a little better now.

LISTENING PLUS

1 **D**=Doctor **A**=Ana
D Come in.
A Hi, Doctor, my name's Ana Martinez.
D Take a seat, Ana.
A Thank you.
D How can I help you?
A Well, I broke my arm when I was on vacation last year.
D How did it happen?
A I fell when I was getting out of the shower.
D Really?
A Yes, the thing is, that happened five months ago, but my arm started hurting again.
D Oh, I'm sorry to hear that. When did it start hurting?
A When I was carrying a new sofa up the stairs.
D Hmm ... that isn't good. Maybe you should get an X-ray. Let's see what we can do.
A Thanks.

2 **M**=Max **Mr. T**=Mister Thomson
M Mr. Thomson, can I come in?
Mr. T Oh, hi, Max. Yes, come in.
M Ouch!
Mr. T Are you OK?
M Not really, no.
Mr. T What's the problem?
M Well, before I came to work here, like, last year, I sprained my wrist.
Mr. T How did you do that?
M I fell off a ladder when I was cleaning windows.
Mr. T I see.
M The thing is, I think I just sprained my wrist again.
Mr. T When?
M Ten minutes ago. I was walking down the stairs, and I missed a step and fell down. Same wrist. And it really hurts now.
Mr. T You can't work like that. You should go home and rest.
M Thanks.
Mr. T Come back tomorrow.
M OK. The thing is, it really hurts. Can I take two days off?
Mr. T Max, come back tomorrow. OK?
M OK.

3 **A**=Amy **J**=Jon
A Hello, I'm Amy.
J Hi, I'm Jon. I'm one of the instructors.
A Nice to meet you.
J Have you been canoeing before?
A Well, I took some lessons on my vacation last year.
J Oh, how was it?
A Oh ... it was fine, but I didn't actually do much canoeing.

J Why not?
A Well, on the first day, I cut my knee very badly when I was carrying my canoe up a hill.
J Ouch!
A My instructor was amazing. He carried me up the hill and took me to the hospital.
J That was nice of him.
A Yes, very nice. In fact, we're married now.
J Wow!
A But I haven't been back in a canoe since then. And I don't know why, but I'm a little scared now.
J OK. Maybe you should go out with someone more experienced today.
A Good. I'd like that.
J And don't worry. You'll be fine.

UNIT 10 LISTENING p. 67

1 **C**=Carl **F**=Franco

C Hi, my name is Carl Rossi. I'm 24 years old, and I live in California. I'm making an audio history of my family. I'm going to talk to my dad and my grandfather to find out what they used to do when they were younger. First of all, my dad, Franco Rossi. Hi, Dad.
F Hi.
C Welcome to the Rossi family history recording.
F It's nice to be here.
C OK, let's start. Dad, where were you born?
F I was born in Italy.
C And when did you come to live in the United States?
F We came here when I was three years old.
C How long ago was that?
F Well, I'm 52 now, so it was 49 years ago.
C And did you come from Italy to California?
F No, when we came to the US, we first lived in New Jersey, and then in New York City. We came to live in California right after you were born.
C What did you use to do in your free time when you were a kid?
F I used to make model airplanes.
C Really? Do you still have them?
F I'm afraid not. And I used to collect stamps.
C Ah, right, I've seen the books. They're amazing!
F Yes. I don't understand why your generation doesn't collect stamps ...
C Yeah, well. Did you use to have a TV in those days?
F Yes, I used to watch cartoons all the time when I was little. Later, I used to watch a lot of comedy shows.
C You didn't have computers, cell phones, or things like that, right?
F No, nothing like that.
C So, what else did you do in your free time when you were a teenager?
F Well, lots of things. I used to go dancing, go to the movies, or just hang out with friends.
C Oh, right, well, teens also do that these days. Did you use to hang out at the mall?
F Well, there weren't any big shopping malls in New York City in those days.
C Oh.

2 **C**=Carl **G**=Giorgio

C Hi, this is Carl Rossi again, and I'm back with my grandfather, my dad's dad. His name is Giorgio Rossi. Hi, grandpa!
G Hi, Carl.
C Welcome to the Rossi family history recording.
G OK, OK! Let's do it!
C So, Dad told me that he was born in Italy. Were you born there, too?
G Yes, I was.
C And did you go to school and stuff there?
G Yes, I did. We lived there until I was nearly 30 years old.
C And how old are you now?
G I'm 79.
C So, did you use to have a TV when you were a kid?
G No! I didn't even see a television until I came to the US.
C Then, what did you use to do in your free time?
G Lots of things! We lived near the sea, so we used to go to the beach a lot. Or we used to play soccer in the street or go for long walks. One of my favorite things was climbing trees. There was a big tree outside my bedroom window. I used to climb down it to go and play with my friends.
C And did you use to hang out at the mall with your friends?
G Carl, they didn't have shopping malls where I lived. They didn't even have supermarkets.
C No supermarkets? So where did you go to buy food?
G We used to go to stores or markets. Or we bought it from farmers.

LISTENING PLUS

C=Carl **S**=Silvana

C This is Carl again. Now I'm talking to my grandmother, Silvana. Welcome to the Rossi family history recording, and thanks for helping me with this, Grandma.
S No problem, Carl.
C OK. Well, I want to ask you about your life in Italy, before you came to the US.
S What do you want to know?
C Well, first of all, when did you meet grandpa?
S We met when we were children.
C Really?
S Yes. We used to live in the same village. In fact, your grandfather lived on the same street. He used to walk past my house on his way to school.
C How old were you when you met him?
S No idea! He was always there.
C Did you use to walk to school together?
S Walk to school with a boy? No way! My parents didn't let me talk to any boys on the street.
C They didn't? Even when you were a child?
S Yes, especially when I was a child. The boys in my village were terrible. They used to get into trouble all the time. Anyway, I didn't like boys in those days. But the girls were nice, of course.
C Tell me about your school.
S Well, it was a small village, so there was just one school for all the children.
C All the children? Until they went to college?
S Yes, but not many people went to college. I left school when I was ... I can't remember, when I was 13 or 14.
C Wow. That's very young to leave school.
S It was normal in those days. Girls didn't use to stay in school for a long time. We had to work at home.
C Work at home? Doing what?
S Housework! Carl, remember, we didn't use to have washing machines, dishwashers, vacuum cleaners. We didn't even have running water! There was a lot of work. Too much for my mother.

C I see.
S Also, I was the only girl in the family, so I used to do everything.
C But you had three brothers. Didn't they do any housework?
S Oh, Carl, did the boys do housework? That's funny!
C What's funny? I don't understand. You had three brothers, right?
S Right.
C And they didn't use to help with housework?
S Right.
C So what did they use to do?
S I told you! They used to get into trouble!

UNIT 11 LISTENING p. 73

I=Interviewer D=Doctor White

I Good evening and welcome to *World Watch*. In the studio with me is Doctor Helen White, who is here to talk about single-use plastics. Good evening, Doctor White, and thank you for coming on the show.
D Good evening. It's a pleasure to be here.
I So first of all, Doctor White. Single-use plastics. What's the problem?
D The problem is very simple. People use too much plastic and throw it away. They don't recycle enough.
I So we're creating mountains of garbage.
D That's right. And people also throw tons of plastic into the oceans.
I Oh, right. Is that a big problem?
D It's a *huge* problem. Imagine a garbage truck full of plastic. We throw that much plastic into the ocean every *minute.*
I That's terrible.
D And it's getting worse. If we continue throwing away plastic like this, there will be *eight million metric tons* of plastic in our oceans by the year 2025. That's like having two hundred bags full of plastic along every meter of coastline in the world!
I What happens to the plastic in the ocean?
D Fish eat it. And then, of course, we eat fish. If you eat fish, you're probably also eating plastic.
I So, is your message—stop using plastic?
D No, not at all! Plastic is very useful. The problem is *single-use* plastic. Things like water bottles, straws, plastic bags. In the US, they buy a million plastic water bottles *every minute.*
I Seriously?
D Yes! And they use five hundred million straws every day.
I That's bad!
D And listen to this. The average American uses more than five hundred sandwich bags a year.
I Five hundred? That's impossible.
D But it's true. And they only recycle about one percent of it.
I Only one percent?
D Yes.
I So what message do you want to give the listeners tonight?
D The message is clear: if we continue to buy single-use plastic items, we will have mountains of plastic garbage everywhere, but most importantly in the oceans.
I Is there anything we can do?
D Yes, there is.
I OK, time for a break. When we come back, Doctor White will have some suggestions about how to make things better.

LISTENING PLUS

I=Interviewer D=Doctor White

I Welcome back to *World Watch*. I'm with Doctor Helen White, an expert on plastic waste. So, Doctor White, we've had the bad news; now let's have the good news.
D OK, well, it isn't good news, but it *is* common sense. If we want to save the planet, we have to change our habits. First of all, water bottles. If people want to buy mineral water, they need to have reusable bottles.
I Reusable bottles?
D Yes. Bottles we can use again.
I I get that. But the water in the store is already in a bottle.
D Right. That has to change. If supermarkets want to continue selling mineral water, they will have to put it in larger containers. Then we fill our own bottles from the container.
I Isn't that a little complicated?
D Let me remind you—in the US, we buy a million plastic water bottles *every minute*.
I OK. Any other ideas?
D Straws.
I What about them?
D Stop using them. If someone offers you a straw with your drink, give it back.
I What if you like using a straw?
D Then you can use your own. If you really want to use a straw, there are stainless steel straws. Buy some!
I Seems like a good plan. OK, Doctor White, we have time for one more idea.
D OK. Don't use plastic bags in a supermarket. Take your own bags. Not plastic ones. Take a good strong reusable bag. They last forever!
I Good one. OK, that's all we have time for. Doctor Helen White, thank you for coming on the show.

UNIT 12 LISTENING p. 79

1 H=Host J=Jim

H Hi, and welcome to *WISP Student Radio*. You're with me, Lucy Lockwood, and today's topic is studying away from home, and I mean really away from home, studying in a completely different country. With me are three students who all have amazing plans to study abroad next semester. First of all, Jim McCormick. Hi, Jim!
J Hi, Lucy.
H What are you studying?
J I'm studying engineering.
H And I understand your special interest is space technology.
J That's right. And next year, I want to study in a country where they have a space program.
H So where do you plan to go?
J Well, the three countries I can choose from are Russia, China, and India. I don't know much about the Indian program, but I think the Chinese program is the most interesting.
H Where is it?
J It's in Sichuan Province, in the southwest of China. But it's very popular. I may not get an invitation to go there.
H I see.

J So I think I'll have a better chance of going to Russia, so I applied for a visa.
H Where's the space program in Russia?
J It's in Star City. It's the place where the Russian cosmonauts go for training.
H And you're planning to go next semester.
J Well, I have to get a visa first.
H And when will you find out if you have one?
J I may have to wait for a few months yet.
H Oh! Not good! Well, best of luck, Jim.
J Thank you.

2 H=Host M=Megan

H And now, welcome to my second guest, Megan Kirk! Hi, Megan!
M Hi Lucy.
H What's your major?
M Information Technology, but my special interest is audio production.
H Oh, I see. What kind of career do you plan to follow?
M Well, I may become a music producer. That's what I hope to do.
H And what are your plans for next semester?
M Well, I'm hoping to do an audio production course in London, England.
H Really? Why London?
M Because they have some great music studios there.
H I see. So, have you applied to do a course?
M Yes, I have.
H Have they accepted you?
M Not yet. And I'm checking out if I can afford to live in London. It may be too expensive.
H And if you can't go to England?
M If I can't go to England, I'll study here in the US.
H Right! We have some good studios, too!
M I know that. I just really want to live in London for a semester!

3 H=Host R=Richard

H And my third guest is Richard Donovan. Welcome, Richard.
R Thanks, Lucy. Nice to be here
H So, Richard, what are you studying?
R I'm studying fashion design.
H I see. And where are you going next semester?
R Well, it may be Italy. And it may be France.
H Where in Italy?
R Milan. It's the center of the Italian fashion trade.
H I see. And what are you planning to do?
R I want to work as an intern in a fashion house.
H Nice! How are you planning to do that?
R Well, my mom has a contact, someone who works in a really amazing fashion house.
H Oh, that's good. So are you going to work there?
R I might. It hasn't been decided yet.
H And what about Paris? Does your mom also have contacts there?
R No, she doesn't. But if I can't work in Milan, I will definitely go to Paris. Milan is the center of fashion, but Paris is also pretty cool.
H Well, very best of luck, Richard.
R Thank you.
H OK, time for a break. Back soon!

LISTENING PLUS

H=Host N=Nancy J=Jim S=Sam M=Megan R=Richard A=Anita

H Welcome back to *WISP Student Radio*. I'm with Jim McCormick, Megan Kirk, and Richard Donovan. Jim, we have a caller who wants to give you some advice. Go ahead, caller.
N Hi, Jim. My name is Nancy.
J Hi, Nancy.
N Hi. I live in Boston, and I'm also studying space technology. Last year I was in China. In Sichuan Province.
J Wow. How was it?
N Just amazing. If you get the chance, you have to go.
H That's very interesting, Nancy. How did you do that? I mean, how did you organize your visit?
N My college organized it for me. Do you think your college can help you?
J Hmm ... they may.
H Nancy, do you have any other advice for Jim?
N Yes. Learn Chinese before you go. You may find it difficult, but you really need it!
H Hello, caller, you're through to Megan Kirk.
S Hi, Megan. My name is Sam.
M Hi, Sam. Nice to meet you.
S Hi. Nice to meet you, too. You want to go to England, right?
M Right.
S You made the right decision. I studied audio production in London, and I had a fantastic experience!
M London is good, huh?
S It's great. The music scene is awesome. There are musicians from all over the world.
M That's great.
S But ...
H Uh-huh, there's a "but."
S There is a big "but." London is a very expensive city. Accommodation is very expensive. Try to share a place with someone.
H Thanks for your advice, Sam!
M Yes, thank you.
S You're welcome!
H I'm with Richard Donovan, who wants to study fashion design in Milan or Paris, but he may need to look at other options. Right, Richard?
R Right.
H Callers, any ideas? OK, we have a caller on Line 2.
A Hello!
H Hello. And your name is ... ?
A Anita Cummings.
H And what do you do, Anita?
A I work in a fashion house in San Francisco.
H Sounds good. So, what do you want to say to Richard?
A Hello, Richard. Italy and France are great, but I have another suggestion. Why not go to Japan?
R Japan?
A Yes. They have great fashion designers there.
R Yeah, you're right.
A I spent a year working in a fashion house in Kobe, and I learned a lot.
R That's very interesting. I'll definitely think about Japan.

VOCABULARY

UNIT 1

camping
go on vacation
go swimming
go to the beach
go to the mountains
hiking
kayaking
rock climbing
scuba diving
sightseeing
stay at a hotel
stay home
surfing
take a vacation
travel somewhere
visit museums
whitewater rafting

beach resort
campground
forest
hostel
hotel
river

acting class
art class
Chinese class
comedy club
fun
semester

athletic
cable
experience
frightening
heights
platform
swing
valley
zip line
zip-lining

UNIT 2

action movie
animation
blockbuster
Bollywood
documentary
horror movie
martial arts movie
musical
romantic comedy
science fiction movie
classical music
country music
jazz
rap
rock music
soul music

annoyed
annoying
amazed
amazing
bored
boring
dangerous
disappointed
disappointing
excited
exciting
frightened
frightening
funny
interested
interesting
relaxed
relaxing
surprised
tired
tiring
violent

act in a movie
direct a movie
famous
play in a band
record a song
tour with a band

actors
comedy show
concentrate
extra
impressed
review
stunt performer
trailer

UNIT 3

BASE jumping
BMX bike racing
bungee jumping
cave diving
clean the windows
do the laundry
drive a race car
drive a sports car
extreme sports
ice climbing
parasailing
ride a bicycle
ride a horse
ride a motorcycle
run a marathon
skydiving
snowboarding
unusual
whitewater rafting
windsurfing
wingsuit flying

airplane
bag of chalk
brave
breathing
camera operator
crazy
drone
microphone
shot
vertical rock formation

fly in a helicopter
sing in public
take dance lessons
win an award
write a poem

UNIT 4

city
continent
desert
island
lake
mountain range
ocean
rainforest
volcano
waterfall

bad
beautiful
cold
colorful
deep
dry
high
large
popular
small
tall
Africa
Antarctica
Asia
Australia
Europe
North America
South America
bike lanes
electric bus
green space
highway
hydroelectric dam
onshore wind farm
passengers
renewable sources
urban rail system

UNIT 5

balloons
birthday
bouquet
cake
candle
card
cathedral
celebration
church
fireworks
flowers
get dressed up
karaoke
New Year's
present
ring
Spring Festival
thank-you card
Valentine's Day
wedding

buckets
celebrate
crops
farming
festival
grapes
harvests
huge
lucky
lucky bags
magic
magnificent
make wishes
mistletoe
monasteries
monks
New Year's Eve
pour
powder
release
spectacular
surprise party
take place
unforgettable
wedding
wonderful

UNIT 6

cook healthy food
eat junk food
eat fast food
exercise
get fresh air
get stressed
go on a diet
go to the gym
indoors
lifestyle
look at screens too much
meal
relax
soda
stressful
take a break
talk on the phone
unhealthy
walk
warm up

meditation
ping pong
t'ai chi

advice
depressed
extraordinary
fail
feel low
feel sick
hang out
headache
negative
optimistic
ordinary
perfect
self-esteem
unfollow

UNIT 7

accessories
bags
boutique
clothing
electronics
jewelry
laptop
mall
pants
perfume
scarf
scarves
stuff

assistant
attractive
busy
cashier
cheap
convenient
crowded
inexpensive
line
loud
noisy
old-fashioned
online
overpriced
reasonable
store credit card
stylish
trendy

consume
furniture
household waste
landfill sites
percentage
pottery
recycled
repair
secondhand
throw away

UNIT 8

a sense of humor
amusing
artistic
athleticism
beauty
elegance
generosity
generous
hardworking
intelligence
outgoing
patient
polite
politeness
reliability
reliable
serious
smart
wealth

interview
roommate
perfect
summer camp

ambitious
avoid
be on time
business major
chickens
connect with
crucial
dress professionally
driver's license
energetic
enthusiasm
evidence
go on a cruise
graduate
house-sitter
impress
impressed
impression
key questions
passionate
pastime
positive
punctual
social media
turn up

UNIT 9

break a hand
break a leg
break an arm
break your wrist
bruise a leg
burn yourself
crash into (someone/ something)
cut your head
dislocate your finger
fall down the stairs
fall off (something)
get a black eye
have a car accident
hurt yourself
hurt your knee
lose a tooth
run into (someone/ something)
smash into (something)
sprain your ankle
trip over (someone/ something)

accident
crime
injury

ankle
arm
finger
hand
head
knee
leg
nose
tooth
wrist

canoeing
intersection
jet-skiing
lose control
perform in front of an audience
reckless
scene
unharmed
waterskiing
witness a crime

UNIT 10

elementary school
high school
junior high school
language school
middle school
primary school
summer school

athletics
choir
drama club
math club
orchestra
ping pong
science club
sports team

act
be in a club
climb trees
collect stamps
dance
go for walks
make models
play a musical instrument
play a sport
play computer games
play in the orchestra
play on a school team
play soccer

play ping pong
plays
watch cartoons
wear a school uniform
win competitions

ancestors
box office
cancel a concert
fans
private school
inspiration
proceeds
saucer
sociology

UNIT 11

air pollution
barista
cardboard tray
continue
garbage
habits
pay bills
plastic bag
plastic cups
plastic spoons
plastic straws
reusable bag
plastic water bottle
reusable cup
survive
waste
your own bag
napkin

glass
metal
metric tons
recycle
recycling center
sandwich bags
single-use plastics
stainless steel
throw away

challenge
clean up
fresh food
green project
green spaces
mainly
oxygen
plant trees
persuade
post a photo online

researchers
solar panels
sort
whole

UNIT 12

applicant
bus driver
good at something
good with something / someone
interpreter
lifeguard
long hours
mailman
park ranger
pay rent
receptionist
sales clerk
server
take a tour
tour guide
travel company
volunteer vacation

audio producer
fashion designer
space engineer
space program
visa

a break
biodiversity
book something
construction work
dive
electronic tag
fascinating
giant tortoise
identify
in danger
library
progam
reef shark
scary
tag
tourism
volunteer